Out of th

Into the Fire

Life on a Remote Greek Island

Paul Delahunt-Rimmer

Published by
Travelleur Publishing
Denby Dale, UK

First published in 2012 by
Travelleur
96 Thorpes Avenue
Denby Dale
Huddersfield HD8 8TB
UK

ISBN 978-0-9556288-6-3

Printed and bound by CPI Group (UK) Ltd, Croydon, CR0 4YY

*Some names have been changed to protect the innocent and
preserve our legal budget.*

Cover image: the village of Stroumbos, Amorgos

To

Henri

Preface

Two hundred and twenty kilometres to the south east of Athens lies the island of Amorgos, the most Easterly Island of the Cyclades. The terrain is rough and rugged with fertile valleys nestling between the mountain ranges. The cliffs plunge from over 500 metres, in places, straight into the clearest, deepest, blue sea one can imagine. The shallower waters are clear and turquoise, lapping onto the golden sandy or white-pebble beaches. The whole island is covered in herbs and wild flowers, which make the mountains a carpet of colour in the spring and a sensory delight as they give off the most wonderful scent in the dry heat of summer. Just 30 kilometres long and 8 kilometres across at its widest, it is the last port of call for the ferries that run from Athens to the Cyclades. It is extremely quiet and free from tourism for most of the year as the uninformed traveller has long since given up on the ship and disembarked at some other island en route. There are a small number of hotels and pensions to stay in, varying in standard and price but there is one particular hotel which is very good for a secluded island with so little tourism. It was this hotel that we initially selected to stay in. The remote location, the excellent walking and the comfortable Cycladic-style of the hotel attracted us to the island in the first place in 1995. For three years we went to Amorgos on holiday, particularly enjoying the peace, quiet and the exceptional friendliness of the people, but most of all the solitude in the mountains and on the many quiet beaches. We particularly liked exploring the old donkey tracks and goat paths that are now rarely used due to the new road which traverses the island.

The caring nature of the island people of Amorgos was evident in the way they reacted to the first tourists. Nikolas tells of a time his grandmother first saw tourists in Langada, a very rare sight in those days. She immediately grabbed them by the arm and steered them into her house. Her hospitality was incredibly generous. They were given cold meats, salad, cheese, bread, fruit, cakes and retsina. Of course, they didn't understand Greek and didn't really understand what was going on, but the lady was so charming and insistent that they felt she would be insulted if they turned down her generosity. They were in fact absolutely correct and it still applies today. When her grandson asked her why she took these people in and fed and watered them, she said, 'They were not from the island and they had no family to feed and look after them'. If they had asked her if there was anywhere they could stay the night, there is no doubt that she would have accommodated them; and would have refused a single drachma in return. In more recent times a friend of ours and his girlfriend mistook a private house for a cafeneion. This is very easy to do as some of these establishments are literally the family front room. They walked in through the open front door, made themselves comfortable and ordered drinks. They were a little disappointed with the choice of beverages, but settled for the glasses of wine which were gladly served to them with great kindness. It was only when they tried to pay that they realised their mistake. Of course, there was no question of payment and indeed the owner appeared insulted by the very suggestion. They left with a little bag of cake and fruit which was foisted upon them to see them through the afternoon. Most visitors to Amorgos find this friendly and generous approach alien in the 21st century and wish to reciprocate. It is not expected and money is out of the question. However the secret is to send some photographs of the hosts and their family back to them. They just love these and their houses are full of such souvenirs.

Amorgos, 2011

Chapter I The Planning

Very few visitors to the island get to see the most remarkable sights here, as they have to be visited by donkey or on foot. It is quite extraordinary walking terrain, and a local guide is essential. Some routes are not too difficult to find, but often interesting and fascinating historical sites, of which people are not aware, lurk just around corners. After years of getting lost and losing gallons of blood from scratched legs, and copious research, we were in a position to show other people archaeological sites and ancient routes through the mountains dating back to the 5th century BC. Essentially we had a saleable product for like-minded individuals.

My wife Henri had eight years behind her working in the Royal Air Force as a nursing sister and an air traffic control officer, and a number of years working in civvy street as an anaesthetic sister. I had 16 years of military service as a pilot and a few years in civil aviation. We had come to a point in our lives where we thought a change of tack and a little commercial risk could do us no harm. Like a lot of people, we dreamt about living on the island that was our favourite holiday destination, so in 1997 we embarked on some market research. There was no doubt in our minds about the financial aspects; we knew that it could not produce an income for both of us, for the whole year. However, if in the beginning one of us worked remotely, maintaining our management consultancy in the UK, the other could concentrate on a special interest holiday programme. With Henri's degree in history and background it seemed logical that she should be in charge of the holiday programme so that I could concentrate on other things. In the event I ended up accompanying her on many of the walks.

For a few years, we still had to return to the UK in the winters to earn some 'proper money'. I would do some management consultancy. Henri would work as an agency anaesthetic nursing sister which, given that this is a specialty field, was very lucrative. The figures seemed to add up to at least have a shot at it. In 1997 we embarked upon a two-year marketing project to promote and sell walking holidays on Amorgos. Thirty proposals and many presentations later, we had it down to a short list of four holiday companies. Many contenders were rejected by mutual agreement due to an incorrect product or client fit, given their particular target sectors. One company rejected our proposal and then went behind our backs to launch it themselves using our intellectual property. Their product fell at the first post, due to the lack of detailed information and our network and route knowledge. Other companies wanted 'roughy-toughy' products involving camping and hardship; we had both done our 'roughy-toughy' bit in the services and decided we far prefer hotels. One company wanted us to set up a full picnic lunch for people complete with china, travelling rugs and a choice of wines, we decided that this came under the 'too difficult' bracket considering that many of our lunch stops were located halfway up a mountain, kilometres from the only road. In business terms we had designed a product of focused differentiation. That is, perceived high value to a particular market segment warranting price premium. It wasn't going to be a cheap holiday, but it was going to be something very special, utilising all our knowledge and skills.

We initially settled for just one company, independent with an excellent reputation and many products similar to ours, but not as far afield. Tina, the product manager, came to meet us on the island in June 1998. She was an attractive, petite lady in her late twenties, with a pale complexion and shoulder-length brown hair. The poor lady had been

4

travelling all day, but she looked fit and energetic and had a good sense of humour. Playing on the latter quality, and our determination that she should see as much of the island as possible, we took her on two walks that afternoon. We don't usually stop when we are walking, we just 'go for it'. It was all a bit too much for her and, at the end of the day, she warned us not to kill her clients if her company went ahead with our proposal. On day two we got lost and had to beat our way through some thick undergrowth. She was already dripping in blood and decidedly unhappy when a friendly little wasp, which quite clearly didn't approve of our programme, stung her. We eventually got to our destination, where my resident nurse had to treat her for heat exhaustion brought on by unseasonable temperatures and our usual cracking pace. It was only at that point that she admitted that she had just returned from a long sick leave and was still recovering from glandular fever, hence the pale appearance.

The following and last day of her stay seemed to go a little better; well, putting aside hospitalisation or death, it couldn't have been worse. By this point we'd already checked in with our job centre back home to see if they had any summer jobs for us for the next year. We sat down in a taverna for a drink at the end of this last walk with her and said 'well, when do we get a decision?' and braced. 'I have already decided', she said. Oh well we thought, back to the drawing board. 'We'll take your product on'. Deathly silence, we looked at each other in amazement. She just loved the island, the mountains, the sea and especially the people and thought that her clients would, too. She didn't say she loved us, and considering the constant hassle I gave her company over the next two years about their administrative prowess, or rather lack of it, probably still doesn't; but it didn't matter, we were halfway there.

After two years of research, planning and preparation, all we had to do now was to deliver said product. We were under no illusions; we knew that this was going to be the difficult part. The other small overriding factor was that neither of us would dream of going on a group holiday; we hate going around as a gaggle. How were we going to cope with tourists who, I knew from my airline days, always leave their brains at home or in an airport locker? This was really the deciding factor in the question of who should be in charge of the holiday programme; Henri - Miss Diplomacy, or me - Basil Fawlty. Henri got the job. After two years, the company we marketed through initially was sold. We went completely independent for the year of 2001 whilst looking for another sponsor. In 2002 we switched to another independent operator. This partnership has proven to be even better. We have now had an excellent working relationship with them for over ten years. It is indicative of their confidence in our product that it took us years to persuade them to send someone from the company to see the island; and the managing director has never been.

Chapter II Setting Off

In our first year, 1999, the brochure came out in January. We sold 30 out of the 120 available holidays in as many days and then they started bombing the Balkans. All bookings stopped.

We couldn't believe people's lack of geographical knowledge. They actually thought they were going to be in danger on Amorgos. We went as far as pointing out to people that some parts of the South of France were nearer to the action than our island, and they wouldn't hesitate to go there. They then voiced their concern about landing at Athens airport and the possibility of enemy action in the air. Even the Americans weren't going to get it that wrong.

We had both operated aircraft right up to the Kuwait border during the Persian Gulf War and were quite used to some action. We were planning to get a ferry down from Ancona to Greece straight through all the action in the Adriatic and were quite looking forward to a free air show. Now we had people who wouldn't even book because of this albeit serious, but relatively contained war, light years away. We did some more worst-case scenario, 'what if' calculations and decided it wouldn't be the end of the world if no one came out; we would just have a very frugal six-month holiday and worry about the bills upon our return to the UK. In the event we sold a few more holidays before our departure from the UK in April 1999.

The company vehicle is a 1975 109 series III soft-top safari Land Rover. We had bought it especially for the job. It was custom renovated and reconditioned for us and really looks the business. We took delivery of it some months prior to our departure to ensure its smooth operation before the long journey to the Cyclades; clever move. Day one after delivery it broke down twice. In the morning the accelerator became disconnected and in the afternoon the brakes jammed on – halfway up the M40. After a few more incidents involving doors flying open, trails of oil, fuel and spare wheels across the UK roads and other small problems such as a failure to start, we took it to the main Land Rover dealer in Oxford for an assessment. A mere 31 items needed attention, in fact they wouldn't even let us drive it home it was so dangerous. Thanks to our solicitors, the trading standards office and some very competent mechanics both at the main dealer and our nearby local garage, we eventually had a great vehicle in which to set off for Greece.

We intended to drive across Europe to Italy, cross the Adriatic by sea to Patras and then drive to Piraeus to board the ship for Amorgos. All of our friends said 'what fun', 'great travel adventure', 'I'd love to do it'. We said 'we were not looking forward to it, it is going to be hell', and we were right. At least we weren't disappointed. On day one, 23rd April 1999, we proceeded from our house in the Cotswolds to Lyon in 17 hours. Our house in the UK was in the countryside on a hill, with views for kilometres across the Blenheim Estate near Oxford. It is 300 years old and built in stone with walls one metre thick. It has inglenook fire places and oak beamed ceilings. Set in considerable grounds with fruit, vegetable, and herb gardens and a small croquet lawn, it was very different to our destination accommodation.

Day two saw us go from Lyon to Parma in 10 hours. This was through what we believe to be absolutely spectacular scenery of the Alps; unfortunately it was pouring with rain and the cloud was so low it was only just clearing the canvas roof of the Land Rover. Day three was Parma to Ancona, that took 5 hours, then on to Patras by ship, which was a 19-hour passage. We were deaf, pretty dumb to have done it, and shaken to bits, but at least we made Greece, in one piece, although it didn't feel like it.

Oxford to mainland Greece by Land Rover in 3 days, with a bit of help from the Chunnel train and Superfast Ferries from Italy to Greece, we thought was pretty good. We would have to wait a day on the mainland for a ferry to Amorgos, but planned to be on the island at 'crack of sparrows' Sunday morning. The Superfast ferry from Ancona to Patras was only a few months old, massive with all mod cons - casino, pool, restaurants, shops and loads of bars! It has many car decks for nearly 1,000 vehicles, and it loaded juggernaut after juggernaut for hours. It even catered for these lorry drivers by giving them their own lounge, waiter service, excellent looking food and also showed adult movies. Henri wouldn't allow me in, saying that a Land Rover is not a lorry, but she hadn't tried fighting with the heavy steering in this overloaded vehicle for the previous two days. We hadn't booked anything apart from the channel crossing, not knowing when we would make each critical point, so in Ancona we just went to the booking office and asked if there were any places and cabins left for that day's sailing. There were, and we were asked what class of cabin we would like. By this time we were not in the mood to rough it, so we just said 'the best'. It turned out to be a luxury grade cabin just one below a suite and it was fantastic. We set up an office in there and caught up on all our e-mails via our mobile phone and laptop computer and got our money's worth by sleeping for nearly 12 hours.

All the work done on the Land Rover before we left seemed to have paid off. It went stealth just before Dover by switching off all its lights. The navigator and pilot had the kitchen sink, but had forgotten the night vision goggles. The RAC were called straight away and then we decided to try some DIY. A panel was ripped off the dashboard and loads of wires twisted together and this seemed to do the trick. There was a funny burning smell but we decided to ignore it. A new switch was fitted in Lyon. We thought that this would be an ideal opportunity to try some of our new credit cards, which had been obtained for this operation. I proudly pulled out my shiny new company Visa Business Card. It was swiped through the machine, gently, at my request, so as not to scratch it, and I wrapped it back up in cotton wool and tucked it away. The machine clicked and whirred a bit and said Non! Henri removed hers from its wrapping, into the machine and Non! Out came the tatty old Amex; Non! Personal Visa; Non! Personal MasterCard; Non! In the end Henri paid with a Euro cheque. For an operation that was based on the premise that all liabilities incurred abroad would be settled through our business cards, this was not a good start. We also went lame just outside Ancona with a slow puncture. We tried putting a bit more air in it at a garage and it then decided to thank us by having a very fast puncture. We managed a tyre change with the assistance a very helpful Italian garage. The mechanics saved us from extracting the kitchen sink etc from the Land Rover to get to the jack. They even pointed us in the direction of their private washroom to get the grease off our hands and offered us grease busting compound, soap and clean towels. Well OK, this was all offered to Henri, but I tagged along and benefited from the inherently high level of Italian male testosterone. With only about 200 kilometres of driving left to do, thank goodness, we considered that we'd had our ration of incidents.

We thought that one wellie change on Larry the Land Rover was enough for one journey and with two spares, one on the bonnet and one on the back, we were not concerned. But no, 125 kilometres short of Athens, on mainland Greece, Larry decided to throw another shoe. There is about 70 kilometers between tyre repair shops and 15 kilometers between turn offs and this was 19.00 in the evening. Someone was looking after us, it seemed. 'Henri the navigator' had a familiar ring to it, but after she managed to navigate us fault free across Europe, she had certainly earned the title. She looked at the map to find a turn off marked 100 metres ahead and a tyre repair place just around the corner. This garage seemed to be open as long as someone was in need. We were not carrying very much cash, so it was a relief to note the Visa sign on the door. The two mechanics had just broken off a big job on a lorry to deal with a couple of British chaps who had limped in under similar circumstances to us. They then, for some inexplicable reason (maybe again it was because I had the duty bird in tow) broke off that job to do ours. After one hour of labour and a few spare bits they had finished. We still have the problem of having learned most of our Greek on Amorgos and have difficulty in understanding people from the mainland. When we speak to them it's probably like putting an islander from the Outer Hebrides in the middle of Oxford; they just look at us blankly. We didn't understand how much all this work was going to cost us, so I just proffered our credit card. Again, there was much throwing back of heads (meaning 'oxi' or no). We pointed to the sign on the window; it made no difference. They still treated us as if we were crazy people from outer space. We tried MasterCard, Barclaycard and America Express all solicited the same 'oxi'. After a few more frustrating minutes we went back to trying to establish the price to see if we could scrape enough cash together. The problem then immediately became apparent; they only wanted to charge us the equivalent of £5 for both tyres. We gave them an extra few drachmas for some beers and left contemplating the possibility of setting up a business from the UK exporting tyres for repair. We looked back to see them start again on the British car. We met the Brits again the following day and found out that they had just missed their ferry to Crete because of the delay. We had a beer with them in Piraeus and they seemed to be perfectly relaxed about the whole thing. They were diving instructors going to Crete for the summer and had left their wives and children back in the UK. Now that's what I call career planning.

How do you get an Athens taxi driver to respect your presence? Preferably drive a JCB or a tank, but the second best thing seems to be a Larry. The other advantage is if you miss a turning in busy Athenian traffic, you just turn the wrong way up a slip road towards a dual carriageway, slip it into low ratio and four-wheel drive, mount the curb, go across the no-man's land through the scrub, under the overpass, down the curb, back into high ratio and up the originally missed slip road in the right direction. Q.E.D.

Our big long wheelbase Land Rover is 1.93 metres high. According to our research on the Superfast ferry this is just 3 centimetres over the limit for a 'jeep'. For just 3 centimetres we declared it as 1.90 metres and hoped that it wasn't too critical where they parked us. It wasn't. It was still a very expensive crossing though, at £300 all in, admittedly on account of our choice of a luxury cabin. I didn't know the limit on domestic ferries, but went into the booking office at Piraeus to book it onto the ferry for its maiden passage to Amorgos, declaring it as a small jeep. Unfortunately in my tired and emotional state, I had parked this very prominent large white Land Rover, which was already attracting some attention, right outside his open door. The ticket agent looked over his glasses out of the door and asked if this was the 'small jeep'. I had to confess it was. He started to root out numerous papers from untidy drawers full of cigarette packets and fag ends to try and establish the vehicle's classification for payment purposes. Sheaves of papers were produced and there was much sighing, slurping of coffee and cigarette smoke. In the interests of his health I said that I could save him a lot of effort by assuring him that it had been going backwards and forwards to Amorgos on these ferries for years and it had always gone as a jeep. He seemed very relieved, I felt that I had done my good deed for the day and he issued us the tickets for just £45 for the 10-hour journey. It was a big difference in price from the previous ferry we'd taken.

We decided to top up the gear oil on the quay at Piraeus, as the garage in the UK had advised us that it was losing some oil and would require regular attention. We put in a litre and it spewed back about ¾; perhaps it wasn't really required. We then moved Larry to another lane and looked disdainfully at the big pool of oil some inconsiderate person had left on the quay for someone to slip in.

Chapter III The Arrival

We arrived in Katapola, the main port of Amorgos, nearly an hour late at 04.00 am. Our vehicle was jammed behind a number of large lorries all of which moved in due course except for the one directly in front of us. Knowing that the ferries do this kind of operation day in day out, we were not concerned, as we knew they had a cunning plan. Because Amorgos was the last island on the run before turning around and going back to Athens, by now, all the vehicles except us and the lorry had disembarked. They started to load for the return, just a few cars and a few people. I wandered nonchalantly to the ramp and pointed our vehicle out to the deck officer. I then noticed that they were preparing to raise the ramp and return to Athens. The Greeks are usually pretty laid back about things so I realised that something was not exactly going according to plan when the officer ran the full length of the car deck to check I was not pulling an amusing little British jape. On seeing we genuinely were not doing a round trip, just for the fun of it, he ran back to the ramp to stop the departure. 'Quick' he said, then he rushed us to our vehicle and directed us out of a very tight spot by much waving of arms and an element of panic. I'm not sure if we drove the back wheels off the ramp or the ramp was whipped away from under them as the ship pulled away from the quay but either way, 'The Eagle had Landed'.

We had to drive to the other end of the island where our operation is based. It was 45 minutes of hairpin bends with a top heavy, overloaded Land Rover in the pitch black. When we arrived in the other port of Aegiali, Henri had to spend a fun 10 minutes hunting for our house key in the predetermined plant pot outside a friend's taverna. We later discovered they had stayed open until only half an hour previous in order to greet us, but unfortunately we were late.

'Hunt the key' was however not half as much fun as 'hunt the house'. We had been there once before but in daylight. We knew to drive to the small quay at Agios Pavlos, a very small old fishing community 5 kilometres outside Aegiali. We then knew to take down a fence over a gap in the wall and drive across two fields. Climb over a wall, negotiate a dried riverbed and, hey presto, there would be the gate to our patio. We found the fence, we found the field, and as is normal in this area the field was terraced. We found a terrace, we found a house; but it wasn't ours. It was too near to the track and not on the beach, where ours was located last time we saw it. We didn't fancy going over a terrace in the Land Rover in the dark so we backed up and decided to try it on foot. Thirty minutes, four terraces, one vineyard and three walls later, we found the dried riverbed. Two hundred metres of scrub negotiated and we were home. There was no way we were moving from there until it was light. An hour later we took the five-minute stroll back to the vehicle, the easy way this time and drove it along the correct terrace.

The owner had done a sterling job of doing up the rooms and apart from a bit of furniture moving, all that was required was to move all the kit from the Land Rover, climb over the wall, cross the dried river bed to the accommodation. Five hours and many aching muscles later, we were in. The next day thanks to Yin Yang MSM muscle easing cream, we were both able to limbo dance with ease, which is amazing as we've never been able to limbo dance before.

Our accommodation was just a hop, skip and a jump from the sea, an idyllic setting. When we had been to look at it the previous year, we were offered one of two rooms, each with an outside bathroom attached. We really needed both. One we would use as an office and bedroom, the other as a kitchen and living room. They were identical and the same price. Now, logic would dictate that one would get discount for renting both. No, the price was higher! The only reason for this, as far as we could see, was that if we could afford two, we were pretty well off and could afford to pay more. Anyway, the whole setup was ideal for us. Our living room was next to the bedroom cum office, but up some steps on a higher level. This gave that room the office roof as a patio. At the lower level, the office had a small garden outside with a gate onto a path leading down to the beach. They were both very basic and simply furnished, but what a fantastic and quiet (or so we thought) location. Just along the beach was a small quay with a few fishing boats.

Chapter IV Setting Up

We went into Katapola to open a bank account at the only bank on the island, The Agricultural Bank of Greece. If we had known it was going to be such a traumatic affair for all concerned, we wouldn't have bothered and would have just stuffed used bank notes under a dead goat or something. The Bankers Draft in Greek drachma which we had drawn on the Commercial Bank of Greece was no good; it had to be either cash or travellers cheques. After a little bit of reasoning and a big staff conference, they decided that they would reluctantly take it. We had to provide everything from Godmother's hat size to the name of the midwife who delivered each of us. Undeterred, we answered all of their silly questions and ignored all the sighing, puffing and panting over a double-barrelled name when the cashier's own name was something along the lines of Ginakokupalotofnothingou. We left the bank with our very own passbook, saying that we had deposited a sum of money with them. We would not be able to touch it for another week, however, until they would be able to ascertain that the Commercial Bank of Greece would pay them. We were not allowed a cheque book, because we were foreigners and could not be trusted (or write in Greek), and they would not pay us any interest on our dosh. Why did we bother? In fact, we found out later that we do get interest on this deposit account and it is actually quite generous.

We got outside to find people bobbing about in the bay. The new vehicle in town (cars were a relatively new development on the island, much to the delight of the donkeys) had created such a stir that they were too busy gawking to remember where the edge of the harbour was; and the Greek Orthodox Church doesn't offer classes in walking on water.

Packed in the back of Larry was an inflatable inshore rescue boat, which seated eight, and outboard engine. It had been on order for months and we had dragged it all across Europe, so we were now jolly well going to use it. The aim was to memorise all the 'destructions' and then put it together as if we were used to doing it every day of our lives. The back-up was to pick a time of day when the two or three resident fishermen were out at sea and have the operating manual and instructions on the side. We went for the latter plan, but did not bank on two French ladies being in the vicinity. They came across from the beach to the quay, and said, 'when are you going back into the village? Perhaps you could give us a lift'. We explained that we lived by the beach and we weren't going back into the village and suggested that they should start walking now or they would miss the last bus back to Chora. We didn't think there was one at that time of year, but it got rid of them. Putting the boat together and inflating it actually went very well. It was a smooth launch off the small quay, but the engine was a bit of a struggle to fit due to the weight. We (all right, I) had a bit of finger trouble starting it; the start sequence to the space shuttle is easier; and then off we went. Being a brand-new engine it had to be run in. This involved three minutes at idle, ten at half-speed and fifty at three-quarter speed with one minute of full speed allowed every ten, got it? Idle no problems, half-speed a bit bumpy with slight swell, and at three-quarter speed we were nearly supersonic and very bumpy with occasional airborne sections (we are qualified in this). Then it was time for the full-speed trial. Have you ever hit a speed bump at two hundred kilometres per hour in a rubber car? I managed to hang on to the engine with one hand and the boat with the other. Henri wasn't so lucky!

The following day the sea was 'dead' calm and sun 'dead' hot; ideal weather to play with the new toy. We took it around to Katapola, the main port on the island, and found some great secluded sandy bays to hide away in for the short tourist season of mid-July to the end of August. Katapola is a very protected bay and was used by the pirates in the region as their base up until 1835, when they were driven off the island. On our return to Aegiali, we went up to the hotel to do what should have been thirty minutes of business setting up a system of payment for the year and left three hours later. They tried every trick in the book to get extra funds out of us for our clients. Who is going to pay for them to occupy their rooms four hours before the normal check in time (when they are empty anyway)? It will of course be three percent extra if you are paying by credit card, can't you take your card and get cash with it for us? We changed hotels the following year. Following this 'business' we then went up to the mountain village of Tholaria to familiarise ourselves with the layout, as our walking programme included a tour of this delightful mountain village.

Aegiali is at the north eastern end of the island and consists of three main villages: Tholaria to the north, which gets its name from the area's Roman arched tombs, 'tholos' meaning arch: Langada to the south, where there is evidence of an early-Cycladic acropolis; and Ormos, meaning cove or bay, which is on the coast where the harbour is now located. Tholaria is a particularly attractive village, and as we had been hopelessly lost there on numerous visits we thought it best to maintain professional credibility by learning our way around. It is easier to get lost around some of these little stone paved streets than deep in the mountains. The village is built in the simple Cycladic style where old stands next to new and new incorporates old. The wall of the large village church has a fifth century BC column set into it and a little further up is a very impressive 'kamara', or vaulted passageway, dating back many hundreds of years. Passing through the passageway brings you to the cafeneion and shop 'O Horeftis', which means 'the dancer'. The taverna is owned by Agiris and his wife, Maria, who also kept a shop down in Ormos in the summer, and 'The Dancer' is a very appropriate name for it because they occasionally have the mother of all parties up there. There is music, dancing and even the smashing of plates, which is very rare these days apart from shows put on for the tourists with cheap plates. At O Horeftis it is usually the best china, and the taverna owner just laughs, jokes and joins in. His wife does not! Very few visitors to the island make it as far as this little local haven and it is almost essential to be pretty deft at sign language or fluent in Greek. There are nearly always a few of the village men drinking coffee or ouzo there and inevitably playing Tavli, a Greek version of Backgammon. It is not a good idea to get involved in one of these games unless you understand the game fully, as it is very quick moving, involving an immense amount of noise with the slamming down of the counters and verbal abuse. The noisier the game gets, the bigger the crowd of men becomes, all giving their advice. The ladies? Well, they are running around doing the shopping, hanging out washing, making lunch and serving the coffee and ouzos, of course.

We were walking down to Ormos once when we passed Agiris in his little red pick-up truck heading up to his place for lunch. He slowed down and threw a carton of milk out of the window at us and saying, 'you look as if you need this' and then drove on. His truck should be registered as an historic monument. It has not got a light on it that works; they are all smashed. There is not a panel on it without huge dents in it. I say it is red, but we only know this from the little bits showing through the rust. He is parked when he hits the wall. The truck is frequently being repaired outside the taverna, usually with a big hammer. This involves all of the spectators each giving advice, the most heard phrase being, 'I wouldn't do it like that'. Fortunately official mechanical checks are not required on the island as we do not have an inspection garage. If ever one was built, half the vehicles on the island would be off the road.

The day after we moved into our house, Jorgos, who was one of our neighbours, came round in the evening to see if we had settled in OK. This was very decent of him. He told a few tales of wartime Amorgos. The Italians occupied the island in 1941, and although things were hard and the army requisitioned a lot of food, it was far worse when the Germans took over two years later. Upon their arrival, it is interesting to note that even the Italians took to the hills. In 1943, the Germans did not allow the fishing fleet to put to sea, and that winter it is said that a number of people died of starvation. He told us about a family living on a small island to the north of Amorgos at the outbreak of war whose son was called up to serve in the army. Unfortunately they didn't have a boat or any other means of getting to Amorgos, so it was the policeman's job to row across and get him. It was a bad winter and he had to wait a few days until the weather was good enough to get over and it was then another three weeks until they managed to get back. He survived his national service and lived a very isolated existence on the small island until his recent death. His widow now lives in Ormos and the island they came from is now uninhabited.

During the war when the Germans took over, the islanders felt sorry for the Italians and abhorred the way they were treated. They joined forces and helped each other with the local people helping to hide the Italians. Anyone who looked very closely at 'Stavros' on his donkey tending the goats would notice that it was actually Giovanni dressed in island attire with a cap pulled well over his eyes to hide his distinctive Italian features that lacked the rugged and weather-beaten looks of an Amorgiani. Living this closely with the community and working together for joint survival, romances blossomed. At the end of the war some Italians remained and married local girls. The vast majority however returned to their native land, unable to imagine eking out an existence on this remote and rugged island, even if it did mean leaving their girls behind. Many islanders still remember these times and some of the elderly ladies will confidentially tell you of their lost lovers from all those years ago. Some years ago two Italian men who had been here during the war returned, with their wives, to see the island and the people that had looked after them during those difficult times. One of them actually found his former girlfriend and old flames were rekindled. One evening he was found talking to his old friend, in her house, by her husband. An enormous row ensued and the two eighty three year olds were again forcibly separated as the Amorgiani threw the Italian unceremoniously out into the street and told him to stay away from his wife.

Chapter V Our First Clients

Our first clients arrived that May in 1999. Before they had even arrived, logistical problems arose with the ferries for their return. The Express Hermes had been a very reliable service year in year out for many years, but the service had been taken over by another shipping line. To economise they had combined the Amorgos service with the one to Astypalia. Instead of returning to Athens upon arrival in Katapola, this new service now went off to other islands, called back into Amorgos and then back to Athens just in time for our clients to miss their flight to Heathrow. We then had problems with the ferry inbound, our agents in Athens couldn't get the cabins we required, oh joy.

In preparation for our first clients, the owner of Celini, a little bar on the beach down in the port of Aegiali, arrived from Athens where he spends the winters to take over his café again for the summer. Vangelis is always the life and soul of the party. He's always hyper, dancing in and out of the bar to the music with trays of drinks and food, always smiling and enthusiastic to see you and always very helpful and generous. He looks much younger than his 60 years, he is of medium build and his slight paunch is due to his pretty consistent diet of spaghetti bolognese. He has a full head of brushed back black hair, always neatly trimmed. He lived for his 16 year old dog Deago, which was sometimes mistaken for his little Arab boy 'assistant' who followed him around like a sullen puppy, only this puppy rolled cigarettes for him. The assistant was not much good at anything else though. He was given the job of painting all the chairs in the café, which he achieved at the rate of about one a day if lucky. He really should have got a job at the Morgan Car factory, although we doubt they would be too impressed with his standard of workmanship. Vangelis is a very competent linguist and has always been keen to teach us Greek. The word one week was phitheealalouthatho; try saying that after a few drinks. It is a local plant that flowers in the spring. Translated means 'Snake Flower' and is actually a Dragon Arum (Dracunculus vulgaris). It has a spectacular tall purple flower, but gives off a stench of rotting meat to attract the flies to pollinate it.

We managed to persuade two from our very first group of clients to arrive a day early to alleviate the cabin shortage on the Wednesday night. They were staying in Athens for a few days before coming out here. We faxed them at their hotel with our proposal and after just one day in Athens, they leapt at the chance. We still didn't have a boat scheduled to get any of them back though. This was the biggest problem in our early days. Over the years the ships have become more regular and reliable.

These first two clients arrived in the early hours of the morning. We couldn't have been luckier as we had bribed them with drives into the mountains and boat trips to get them out here early and if they'd turned out to be morons we'd have been pushed to our diplomatic limits for the day. Angela and Martin were absolutely charming.

We needed to go into Katapola to get some money for our landlord, Nikitas, who had turned up the previous day. He had a beer, made an excuse to go into every room (not difficult with just two, plus two bathrooms) and then very kindly put a bamboo cover over our patio area. The bank in Katapola said they still weren't sure if we could have any of our money yet. After seeing 'the look' I gave them, which implied we could call the Turks in on a pre-emptive strike if they didn't give us our money, they were very relieved to be told by the computer that we now had access to our funds. We had also given another British couple and their child a lift into town and met Vangelis there, who was very pleased to get offered a lift back. Little did we know how much trouble these kind gestures were going to cause us. In the afternoon we took Angela and Martin out in our boat to an isolated cove that we had discovered. The previous day we had burnt some of the rubbish that was washed up onto the beach there, so it all looked pretty idyllic. Deep blue, clear water with the sun glistening on it, the rocky sides of the cove plunging vertically down into the depths and a large sandy beach. We offered to leave them there for the day and pick them up later. Martin said, 'the last time we spent a day on a beach was in 1982 and we didn't know what to do with ourselves then'. We were very like-minded as indeed most of our clients turn out to be. We drank a can of beer each and whistled back.

In our initial planning, we had had concerns about how clients would get along, and we had discussed group-bonding techniques as they would be together for two weeks, sometimes in challenging situations. But our first group of twelve turned out to be delightful and exactly the type of people we had hoped to target: lawyers, doctors, teachers, and local government officers, aged from forty-five to sixty five.

We decided to play it by ear and not subject this group of clients to management training techniques on holiday. We did not need to worry. They had met on the aeroplane, travelled together to the port, stayed together in Athens and then spent the night together on the ship. We do not know what they got up to on the ship and if the wives they declared to have upon arrival were the same ones they started with from the UK, but they were the best of buddies when they arrived, we were the outsiders. After our first walk we all went to O Horeftis for a drink. They arranged a large table for themselves, but no seats for us. This was our first problem; we were being treated like the staff and not part of the group. The problem was soon resolved and never repeated.

The previous day they had got stuck in a traffic jam in Athens on their guided tour (we subsequently found out there was a student demonstration, a major football match and a train strike all on the same day). They hated the city, but appreciated a visit to the Acropolis and got a little time to walk around. Their ferry called in at an extra island and was two hours late, they thought the ferry was a bit down market, even the first-class lounge, and they didn't get any sleep. Apart from that they had had a great day. They were a bit grumpy, 'bit' being the operative word. One man (a retired GP) within the first three minutes in the hotel told me that he didn't like the tour of Athens, he couldn't sleep on the boat and his glasses were broken. I was about to tell him I would arrange a bulldozer to raise Athens to the ground before his return journey, on which I would accompany him and sing lullabies all the way and we would get an optician parachuted in from Athens, when Miss Diplomacy stepped in, pity really. He spent the next week not believing anything we said by asking each of us the same question separately to see if we gave the same answer. We later found out that on his return to the UK, he filled in the holiday questionnaire before even unpacking and rushed out to catch the Saturday post. He said we walked too fast. He was in fact grossly unprepared for a walking holiday and others had felt that he was holding them back. He criticized us for not giving them a guided tour of a monastery in which speaking is forbidden and our sign language is a bit rusty. He apparently was unaware that a licence from the Greek authorities is required to be a tour guide in ancient sites. He then said we didn't know the name of a flower. Between us we can offer qualifications in aviation, air traffic control, nursing, business management, history, sailing, even combat survival, but not bloody botany. Of all the clients that year he was the only one we were glad to see the back of. He was in some discomfort on the last walk due to blisters and was discussing with his delightful and long suffering wife the possibility of getting a taxi from the port to the hotel. He obviously thought he was approaching Hyde Park Corner. As luck would have it, a friend was the first person we saw when we got back into civilization and we went over to speak to her in her car as our man limped by. She said, 'would any of them like a lift back to the hotel?' 'Of course not', I replied, 'they are on a walking holiday, they can bloody well walk'.

Our presence was demanded at the police station. We got back from a walk to be told by the hotel that the police had seen us driving people around the island in our vehicle, which we were not licensed to do. They had said, 'this is a job for the bus and for the taxi'. We asked if they thought it was urgent or would it wait until tomorrow. We were assured that it was urgent, so we said we would go straight away. We were informed that this was not a good idea as it was siesta time and waking up Stamatis, the chief, could be detrimental to our well-being. We reported at 19.00 that evening in our best Mediterranean business attire with brief cases. The intended first impression worked. Stamatis was sitting at his desk looking very officious with three packets of bullets lying there which had burst open all over the place. My old armoury sergeant would have had kittens at this slack attitude to munitions control.

Stamatis was a large man with a very round face and thinning hair. He looked as if he had just got out of bed. Which of course he had. We have Greek sign writing on one side of our Land Rover and English on the other. He had only seen the Greek side and assumed we were locals operating an illegal taxi service. He only needed to take one look at us to realize that a mistake had been made. It was then all smiles and cheerful banter, especially when I offered my wrists for handcuffing and promised to go quietly. However to maintain face he said, 'I will send for you again in due course to inspect all your papers.' But he never did, and from then on he just waved to us as he passed by. As we left, we did wonder why he needed all those bullets on such a quiet island, perhaps there was something which took place in the middle of the night that we didn't know about. Perhaps this was the reason we had heard he was asking for a transfer because he found Amorgos too stressful.

We found out some months later that it was in fact something that happened in the early hours of the morning that necessitates all those bullets. It wasn't gun or drug running and it didn't involve a secret mafia hideaway in the mountains but rather one of the young policemen who sometimes got a little carried away on his night rounds. He always called in at all the cafes and tavernas and usually finished at a disco on the beach. He had been known to be there in full uniform and considerably the worse for wear. One night, trying to impress the visiting girls he got onto the dance floor bopping away, waving and shooting his gun into the air to the beat of the music. Fortunately it was an open-air dance floor so there was no evidence, in the form of plaster and light fittings on the ground, apparent the following morning. He just needed to reload his depleted magazine to get ready for the next Saturday night. No wonder the police chief felt stressed.

Chapter VI The Programme Starts

Just after our first clients arrived, in May 1999, the weather was horrendous in the night, with high sea and winds, sea state seven. We went to inspect our boat at its mooring and two warps had broken free. It was jammed under an overhanging rock full of water and being bashed to smithereens by the sea. We fought for three quarters of an hour to get the engine ashore and tried to secure it further up the beach. Every time we got enough water out to pull it up a little bit further, another wave would fill it. We both got knocked down several times and Henri went under the thing once, fortunately she was not too badly hurt, just a grazed knee and rope burns on her hands. Even with the engine off it is too heavy for us to lift or even drag, so every time the swell lifted it off the bottom, we took up the slack on the bowline and secured it as high as we could, just hoping for the best. Our brand-new immaculate boat was now well and truly weather beaten. Looking on the bright side, at least we wouldn't look like the new kids on the sea any more, if we ever got it to float again. Battered and bruised, we met the English couple that we had given a lift to a few days ago. They were at breakfast in the hotel, studying the waves smashing twenty metres up the cliffs with unusual interest. It turned out that they were sailing back that day. I told them they were lucky to be going because one sea state higher and it would be too dangerous for the ferries to sail. That put them off their toast and honey. Henri told them that the very best seasickness tablets are Stugeron, anything else is useless. They were interested as to where they could buy them, as they only had Quells. We assured them that any decent pharmacy stocks them, but not in Greece, any self-respecting person from this seafaring nation would prefer to die rather than to be seen buying seasickness tablets. Even the half-finished coffee was pushed aside at this point. Our clients were a bit livelier that day and we had another short bimble, which took them hours. We returned to find the sea state was now eight Beaufort and saw the very relieved English couple tucking heartily into a large lunch, whilst inspecting the small print on their travel insurance to see if it covered Greek ferry delays.

Our destination for that day was Chorafakia, a peak which stands 823 metres above sea level. But hour by hour, the weather got even worse. The sea state was still eight, but now there was thick black cloud over Chorafakia and the wind was about thirty knots, which gives fifty knots or more on the peaks. When we went to inspect the boat, it hadn't moved too much, but it was full of water again and rubbing on the rocks. There was nothing we could do until the weather abated. That day, May 8th, was a festival day at the monastery of Theologos (meaning voice of God) on the way to Chorafakia, so there was a board meeting. We both decided to go ahead with the walk, visit the festival and then see how far we could safely go through the area of Krikellos on the way up to the peak.

Everyone enjoyed seeing the festival and each of our clients took turns standing in the doorway of the church to see something of the service and listen to the singing. One lady, the GP's wife, got slightly over enthusiastic and stepped inside. A little old lady in black insisted she should take her seat and our client was stuck there for the whole of a half-hour sermon which was delivered in monastic Greek. Quite a clever move on the old lady's part, we thought. We were invited to stay at the monastery for lunch and return later for tea in the farmhouse, but we felt fourteen of us would be imposing a bit and so we slid off. We made it as far as Stavros, which is forty minutes short of the summit, and sheltered there in the festival building and ate a picnic lunch prepared by the hotel. The wind on the path around the cliffs was, in our opinion, just in limits to be safe to lead the party as far as Stavros, but as soon as we got around the corner onto the more exposed mountains it was gale force, very cold and certainly not safe to continue. No one disagreed with our decision; good job really, because 'we' weren't going any further. We returned to the port to find that one of the farmers had been poisoning the domestic dogs along the beach; two were dead and one severely ill. It was not the first time he had done it, but no one could prove anything. There is a law in Greece that states that, apart from when they are working, dogs should not be further than two metres from their owner. Therefore the owners of these dogs that had been wandering around were actually in the wrong. One of the dogs that had been killed was a Labrador that belonged to two little girls who were out of the country at the time, attending the funeral of their father, who had died of cancer. We felt very sad for them. So much for the image of an idyllic and happy remote island.

One day we took our group down to Megali Glifada. There are two Glifadas, Mikri Glifada and Megali Glifada, meaning the little one and the big one. The two bays are down from Tholaria, which is one of the main villages at this end of the island. The villagers also call Mikri Glifada, 'The valley of the doomed donkeys'. This is because in days gone by when donkeys were too old to work they were put down in this valley to die. Although this sounds cruel, in actual fact the islanders are very kind to their animals. They were simply putting their retired donkeys into this old folk's home valley, where there is a good water supply and plenty for them to eat. It enabled them to chat amongst themselves, have a sing along, play tavli and live comfortably for the rest of their natural lives. It is relatively easy to get down to Mikiri Glifada but Megali Glifada is a completely different matter.

There are only a hand full of people still alive who know how to find the very remote, hidden, secret path to the bottom.

For years we had been trying to persuade someone to show us the way, but most of the few who knew were now too old to make it in one piece. Apart from the paperwork involved, it would be jolly embarrassing to be stuck at the bottom of the valley with a corpse on our hands, not knowing the way out. The previous year we mentioned our wish to visit the area to the hotel owner, Nikitas. Unbeknown to us, it turned out that the whole area belongs to his family. His family home is down in that area and as a boy he used to help his father look after the goats in all of these valleys. He had been up and down to the bottom of the gorge more times than he could remember, and as far as he knew his boat house still stood down there. He said that he would show us the way. We would take some food and wine and make a day of it. Unfortunately his wife had the fun detectors out and a massive argument ensued, based around her slaving away whilst he was off enjoying himself. Either she came too, or she would find someone else to take us. Again it looked as if we were never going to discover the secrets of Glifada. A few days later Nikitas announced that the following morning we would go regardless of what his wife said – a very brave man.

Nikitas is one of the most delightful islanders. He is small in stature, but very wiry and strong. His sun-beaten face always features a welcoming smile. At the time we were first setting up our business, he was in his early sixties. On the day in question, we set off at dawn with Nikitas carrying a large bag. Once we got into the mountains, he was off like a shot. We consider ourselves to be fast walkers, but we could hardly keep up with him. He went up and down disused and overgrown donkey paths, over walls and through the bush like a Zulu warrior following the spore of a lion. He stopped at a very remote, uninhabited farmhouse and sat down in the yard. We panted our way through the gate sounding like two small steam engines pulling freight up Shap. It turned out to be his family home. We sat next to him whilst he recollected his youth; he hadn't been back to this house in over thirty years. He showed us where his father, grandfather and uncles used to sit, where the goats were kept and where his mother used to cook. He took us down to a spring deep down in a cave where the water is still pure and cool, even in the heat of the day. We filled all the water troughs for the goats and repaired a few fences. He was visibly upset about the state of disrepair that everything was in and bemoaned the youth of today and how they just were not interested in the land and farming anymore. He showed us a sheer cliff two hundred metres high plunging dramatically into the deep blue ocean below and recounted how his uncle had stupidly gone around the cliff face to rescue a goat that had become stuck. The thought of going onto that cliff unaided brought a shiver to my spine. He didn't elaborate on the story. We only found out a year later that his uncle had actually fallen off and a fishing boat found his body three days later. When Henri, supposedly known as Miss Diplomacy, inquired as to the welfare of the goat, her question went unanswered.

Nikitas then took us to the top of the gorge where you can look down to the beach nearly two hundred metres below. We know most of the island and there are some very dramatic sights to be seen, but this view takes some beating. The sides of the gorge seem almost vertical and drop down into the clear blue water. The waves break onto the rocks in a bright white foam and lap up onto the wide beach below. Eagles circle the mountains above and seagulls swoop and dive down into the waters below. On the opposite side of the gorge is a little cove set into the side of the cliff, a cove within a cove. The smaller cove turned out to have played a role in

World War II. It was here, Nikitas told us, that during the Italian occupation a British commando vessel hid from the enemy.

They couldn't be seen from the sea, and apart from the very remote spot where we were standing, they couldn't be seen from the land. It was a near perfect hiding place. They didn't however bank on the goatherds tending their animals in these almost inaccessible places. They also didn't allow for the generosity of the islanders even when times were very hard, and their propensity for partying. As soon as Nikitas' father and family saw the boat, they gathered freshly baked bread, home produced cheese, goat's milk and raki and went down to greet their allies. No amount of persuasion could stop them from throwing a party on the beach. When the British were finally persuaded that there was no chance on earth that the Italians would find them there, they joined the islanders on the beach. Out came the violins and lautos and the singing and dancing lasted three days. No one, of course, found out what the commandos were doing there or what their mission was, but they seemed to enjoy their three days of unofficial R&R.

Now there was no one in the bay and no one on the beach, not even a German towel in sight. It looked like an impossible task to make your way down the sides of the gorge, but Nikitas showed us the start of a hidden path where they used to take their donkeys down. Step by step, we wound our way down around boulders and past a few disused animal shelters. Halfway down we came across an old, dilapidated, home-built ladder leaning against a cliff. In this virtually unknown place someone had constructed and placed a ladder so that they could pick the buds off a plant. We had seen people clambering around cliffs picking something, but we didn't know what they were after. We found out that these buds are very much sought after because they are from the caper plant (capparis spinosa). If the buds are allowed to flower, they produce a beautiful pink and purplish flower. To prepare the buds you soak them, and indeed some of the leathery paddle shaped leaves, in brine, or pack them in salt for ten days. They are then washed and preserved in vinegar and served with salads. In June the islanders go to all lengths to pick what they call 'kapari' from the cliff faces where they grow. Men hang by their fingertips, in the most precarious positions, with no regard for their own safety. Every year someone falls off; fortunately so far only sustaining broken limbs.

After about forty five minutes we found ourselves on the beach. According to the winds and currents, the beach alternates between sand, gravel and pebbles, and on this day it was pebbles. Nikitas' boathouse still stood and he delved into a hiding place inside to see if a few of his boyhood treasures were still there. They were: a few bottles and bits and pieces and an old joiners wood cutting tool. No 1955 copy of Playboy though. After listening to Nikitas reenact the party with the commandos, and indeed after the walk down there, we felt as if we'd been through a commando training session; Nikitas got out 'breakfast'. He had brought fruit, cheese, eggs, bread and indeed enough to feed a ship's company. The bread he had brought was double baked. This is a technique used on the island that dates back thousands of years and the bread is known as 'paximathi'. Traditionally the families would only get the bread oven going and bake bread every few weeks. Enough would then be set aside for use over the next few days and the rest would be put back into the oven and 'double baked' until hard. These rusks would then be placed into large earthenware pots and sealed. They would keep for many weeks in this manner. When eaten they would be remoistened with water or by dipping into tea, coffee or soup. Before we could stop him Nikitas had thrown the entire bread supply into the sea. Paximathi is not our favourite bread, but we were a little upset about him carrying it all this way just to feed to the seagulls and fish. It did however float and in due course washed ashore. He gathered it up and placed it on the makeshift table in front of us, the whole act apparently being intentional. He took some himself and announced, 'wonderful, moist and salty'. To us it was extremely soggy and tasted like seawater, however the cheese was nice.

The beach is northerly facing and as a result collects a considerable amount of rubbish in the winter. After such a difficult walk it is a little disappointing to come to such an idyllic spot to find it covered in rubbish from ships, so in the spring that year, after our expedition with Nikitas, we spent a day down there building fires and cleaning up the beach. We did ask Nikitas if anyone would mind our noble civic deed (admittedly thinking mainly of our clients) and quite rightly, he said, 'who would know'? Although collecting up hundreds of plastic water bottles, tons of wood, numerous aerosol cans and a surprising number of items from ship's survival kits is not fun, there were some interesting finds. There was a bottle with a cigarette sealed into it, obviously the result of someone preparing for the worst. The top of a ship's doorway with officer's accommodation written on one side and crew accommodation on the other came to light. I took it home, cleaned it up and varnished it. It is now in my study. We found a plastic paged French survival manual telling you everything from how to build an igloo to guidelines on delivering a baby; we would have thought that extra mouths to feed in a survival situation would be the last thing you wanted. Even a water cistern from a toilet was there, really just about everything you would need if shipwrecked. It does make you wonder how some of these items came to be in the sea in the first place. We even found the inevitable bottle with a note in it. It was written in Greek and asked, if found, for the author to be contacted. It had clearly been in the sea for some time, but certainly not centuries, as the mobile phone number was still clearly visible. Obviously in the interests of our own survival we tried to keep the aerosol cans off the fires, as the solution for having a can imbedded in the temple was not covered in the survival manual. Inevitably, however, the occasional can found its way into the inferno and it's amazing how high into the air they fly when exploding.

We still had to get out of that gorge on the first visit with Nikitas. As mentioned, we had descended into the gorge by the means of an old donkey track, and this had taken some time. Nikitas said 'would you like to return the quick way, although it probably will not a be suitable route for your clients?', and this turned out to be an understatement. We agreed that it would be interesting to see another route, but with hindsight this was probably a mistake. We started off the way we had come, but after about 10 minutes, he turned left and shot straight up a cliff face. We clambered and climbed, trying not to look down but to see what he was using as hand and foot holds, and after about another ten minutes we reached the top. We looked down to see the way we had come up and couldn't decide whether to throw up or pass out. He gave us thirty seconds to recover and then shot off again across the bush. The following day we were a little tired, but Nikitas' body had remembered how old it was and refused to move. To this day he accuses 'us' of breaking 'him'. We take all our clients down to Megali Glifada, and they agree that it is a most remarkable walk. We do however do it at a sedate pace and stick to the donkey track.

The weather continued to improve throughout that week in May 1999 and our first clients were finding it harder and harder going. It had been very time consuming looking after them, especially given the difficult ferry schedules. The majority of them left on the Friday, but to get them to Athens in time for their flight we had to charter a small boat from Amorgos to Naxos (at vast expense to our company) and taxis across Naxos. The journey in a high-speed private fishing boat was fun and took one and three-quarters of an hour in perfect conditions. We went with them to ensure smooth connections and witnessed a spectacular sunrise and saw a school of dolphins just by Naxos. Our only other option was to send them back to Athens a day early to spend another day there. It was our first group and generally they were really great people, so we decided to take the expensive option. Not that they seemed to appreciate it; they didn't buy us a single beer the whole time they were here.

Some of our clients had arrived in Amorgos early, some stayed in Athens for different lengths of time and three ferry schedules and transfers were involved. Doing the accounts was a nightmare. Thank goodness for Excel. We have contingency figures built into the costs for ferry problems, but until we had time to work out the exact liabilities and incomes, we had no idea where we stood with this generous gesture of a private boat cruise for our clients. Our books balanced, thank goodness.

Chapter VII Ships and Boats

A day later we took our two remaining clients to Katapola to catch the local boat, the Express Skopelitis, to Naxos, after which they would be transferring to the Seacat to Athens. Captain Skopelitis had this new boat and it was a great improvement on the old one that we had travelled on a number of times. The old one was just called 'The Skopelitis'. The addition of 'Express' to his new one reflected the fact that it went about 2 knots faster.

The last occasion we had used the captain's old service from Naxos to Amorgos, two years earlier in May 1997, we were four hours late, due to having to call in at an extra island way off track. It was billowing more black smoke out of the engine compartment than the funnel, which was concentrating all its effort on spitting out as many sparks and glowing soot as it could manage, and this was supposed to be diesel powered. On another occasion when we were on board, the singing, dancing, violin playing and whiskey drinking on the bridge started in Naxos, and by the time we were an hour out of Amorgos, the crew seemed well out of it. We took a great chunk out of the quay on a small island just before ours due to a slightly over enthusiastic departure procedure. About six people rolled off the bridge to inspect the damage and staggered back in peals of laughter to continue the merriment all the way to our destination. We stayed exactly where we were sitting, on the life rafts!

There was another occasion when the old Skopelitis was running very late, due to a family relocation. Mother, father and two children with all their worldly possessions were on board, expecting to be moved to a remote island without even a quay. The ship was anchored offshore from their destination and rugs, chairs, kettles, beds, clothes and farming implements were all handed down to a small rowing boat and shuttled to the shore. After a considerable length of time the operation was complete, farewells were exchanged and the ferry eventually set off again. After a few minutes a very observant passenger noticed the rowing boat heading after them at a speed that would do a university boat team proud. Someone was standing in the bows waving and shouting. Captain Skopelitis was informed and yet again the ferry came to a halt and the boat pulled alongside. The forgotten toddler was handed over and everyone continued on their way again.

One morning we were in Katapola, waiting for the new 'Express' Skopelitis to depart. The mayor, the policeman, the priest and a few fishermen were all sorting out the problems of the world in a cafeneion on the waterfront in Katapola when we arrived. A few other locals were drinking coffee awaiting the departure. Captain Skopelitis prides himself on timely departures, because that way he is at least on time once somewhere on the schedule, and usually only once. That day, he didn't even make the departure on time, but it would have been an extremely brave seaman to venture out to sea under the circumstances he was facing. The sea state was calm, visibility was perfect, there were no obstructions to hinder his departure and all systems were operating normally; well, as normal as they ever are on his boat. Although in his defence, his was the first ship cleared to sail after all ferries had been stopped for inspection after a major accident. His deep concern was a message that his crewman on the ramp had relayed from an authoritative voice coming from deep inside the grocer's shop beside us. There was a small commotion going on inside and a lot of hasty words being spoken; unusual for Katapola, especially at 07.01 in the morning. We turned, expecting to see the island police frog-march the grocer onto the boat to be taken into custody at headquarters in Naxos. Perhaps it was Lord Lucan, shrivelled and wrinkled after many years in hiding on a remote Greek island. His donkey could easily have been Shergar in disguise. At that moment, our chief priest shot out of the shop, his cassock hitched up with one hand, a loaf of bread under his arm, and in his spare hand he clutched a bag of tomatoes and cheese. The distinctive, tall hat of the Greek Orthodox Church must have a speed limitation well in excess of twenty five knots, because he moved across the quay like an ostrich after an investment opportunity. His opinion of the on-board catering obviously agreed with ours. With all bets hedged against any possible forces of nature or otherwise, the ferry departed four minutes late.

When we got back from Katapola to Aegiali, we were speaking to Vangelis about the ferry problems and how the new 'Express' Skopelitis was a great improvement over the old one. He told us about being on the maiden voyage. 'When we were pulling out of Katapola, the ship went into a holding pattern out in the bay. Round and round it went until the passengers were feeling quite dizzy'. Not being an area of heavy shipping activity and already being about two hours late on schedule this was very confusing to all. 'Suddenly an engineer ran along the deck to the stern with a huge hammer sticking out of his overalls pocket. He disappeared down a hatch and then much cursing, swearing and hammering was heard. All of a sudden the ship lurched out of its now extremely boring manoeuvre and headed in a straight line towards Naxos. The engineer reappeared, now with the hammer protruding from an opposite pocket, to much cheering and applause'.

Following the storms the previous week, after we had seen our first clients away, we had had to move our boat onto dry land until we could get an anchorage set up in the bay by our house. Our neighbour was Titi, short for Christina. She was a delightful, incredibly generous and helpful French lady. She said that she was 55. The fact that her passport listed her birth date as 'D-Day' seemed irrelevant. She was very slim and wrinkled, with obvious signs of excessive smoking and ouzo intake. Her huge mass of thick, grey hair stuck straight up and had a life of its own. She always wore numerous necklaces of varying materials from silver to gold, from cords to leather. Hanging from each one would be reading glasses, driving glasses, pendants, shells and even fishing floats. They were always in a massive tangle and extracting a pair of glasses would be a major operation which would make open heart surgery seem like a stroll in the park.

She insisted on helping us with the boat and got instructions for us from the fishermen as to a good mooring place and anchorage and what we required to achieve this. She helped us get the boat out of the water until we could anchor it properly and we put the engine alongside. I wasn't at all concerned about the security of the engine, but she insisted on putting a small stone on top of it; apparently this indicates that it belongs to someone. The other sign is to lean a possession against a wall. We had actually leant the engine against a wall as well, so this really was belt and braces.

We went to the chandlers in Katapola with a huge shopping list of requirements, compiled by Titi's fishermen contacts. An anchor (even we were able to work that one out), fifteen metres of chain, three 'mannions', which we believe are called shackles in English, fifteen metres of anchor rope, ten metres of mooring rope, a buoy and a swivel joint. The chandlers were closed, but a young chap who ran the shop next door got the key from under the plant pot and let us in. He couldn't speak English, so his mother leaned out from the taverna balcony on the other side and translated. He didn't know anything about boats, so he phoned the brother of the shop owner, who lived close by. The brother came to join the party and was very helpful, but didn't know where everything was. The garage owner across the road sometimes minded the shop, so he was called across to help. At this point an old sea salt came in and understood our requirements precisely. With the mother, the lad, the brother, the garage owner and the old sea captain, we managed to collect everything we needed. Smiles all round, and everyone congratulating each other that they had between them managed to satisfy the 'Brits' requirements. All we needed to do now was pay, easy. Wrong, only the shop owner knew the prices of everything. But fortunately for all concerned, at this point he turned up. With reference to catalogues, rope spool ends, scales brought in from the brother's toilet roll factory next door and labels, we had a price, which was quite expensive thanks to the chain and anchor. Great, Visa proffered as advertised on the door, six faces went blank. It turned out that only the owner's wife knew how to use the Visa machine did we know how? With only their money to lose I was willing to have a go. Card in, paper in, couple of whizzes across with the roller, a few squiggles and we legged it PDQ (well as PDQ as you can go with fifty kilograms of chain and a ten kilogram anchor).

We had to go back the following day to change a bit which apparently wasn't quite right and which had failed the local fisherman's inspection. The Visa charge did actually go through, but it was some two months later.

That week, we had a new visitor to the office. It was a creature called a sarandapothi. This means forty legs, but we have never hung around long enough to count them. It is like a centipede, but about 10 centimetres long and a centimetre across and has a bite which will incapacitate you for many days. As our landlord arrived about fifteen seconds after the discovery, I invited him to dispatch said guest. He didn't do a very good job, all he managed to do was to dissect it in half with an old chair leg. As a nurse, Henri was quite interested in the internal workings of said creature but a chair leg is not exactly a scalpel and the cut was not very neat to say the least. It was also not a very effective way of executing this creature as half an hour after he left, the two parts were still working perfectly well but independently. They were crawling in opposite directions across the middle of the office as if head and tail had decided to get divorced and start new lives apart. Research shows that if a piece of wood fails to work, being tapped heavily on the head with a masonry mallet does the trick.

We had been helping our friend, Michalis, a couple of times by pulling his boat out of the water with our Land Rover. He always kindly repaid us with a few beers at one of the bars near the quay. We had to drive back to our house; usually the hairpin bends and precipitous drops every hundred metres ensures that no one drinks and drives very far. It also provides a free source of spare parts for both cars and people. I did however make an idle inquiry as to the then local policeman's policy on drinking and driving, as after our last meaningful discussion he seems to consider us as his best mates. When the laughter through the whole bar had subsided and people had picked themselves up from where they had been rolling and clutching their sides the policy was explained.

The biggest problem is stopping the policeman drinking and driving; it is the customers and taverna owners who have to stop him, not vice versa. There was one famous occasion when he had to take someone in handcuffs from Amorgos to the nearest police cells in Naxos. He got the 18.00 ferry which was due in at Naxos at 23.00. He didn't make the police station until 06.00 the following morning. As soon as they got on the ferry he headed straight for the bar and, being a very decent man and feeling sorry for his charge, he bought them both a few drinks; well OK quite a few drinks. On arrival in Naxos the attraction of the nightlife in all the bars along the front was just too much and he persuaded his prisoner to keep him company (not much choice given the matching bracelets they were wearing) and so the night seemed to turn into morning. They never did find the keys to the handcuffs.

It must be said that we now have a breathalyser on the island. OK, it doesn't come out of its box very often but our current chief, Costas, takes a very dim view of drinking and driving. He is a very upright slim gentleman always impeccably dressed with smoothed back black hair. He is very religious and the few times I have been into his office I have thought that I had taken the wrong turning and ended up in the police station's private chapel. Icons and religious artifacts abound. No loose bullets rolling around on this desk. Perhaps the odd altar candle though.

Chapter VIII Fishing

In the spring of 1999 we had a chance to go fishing. Titi very kindly offered to take us in her boat and let us into the secrets of this black art. The weather was absolutely ideal: a dead calm sea, clear skies and hardly a breath of wind. We should have set out earlier, but Titi was not good at 'early' and she had been helping us with our ouzo-lake until midnight the previous night. We eventually set off at about 10.00. This fishing thing is an art form that neither of us had practiced before, so benchmarking the starting point was not difficult. We were very keen to learn however, as we do like fish and it is difficult to buy on the island. At that time of year, a lot of the fishermen's catch goes to the restaurants, and anything that is left over goes to the fishermen's families or is used for bartering. If it is a large haul, it is boxed up in ice and sent to Athens, where they can get twice the price for it. The result is that we either have to buy fresh fish under the counter from a friendly restaurant owner, or catch it ourselves; we liked the idea of the second method, as it is a bit cheaper. We asked Titi what we needed to bring with us for this expedition and she told us that she would provide everything. This turned out to not only include the fishing tackle but the breakfast supply of ouzo! The ideal place for catching a particular type of fish was in a bay on the island of Nikouria opposite to our house.

It took us about three minutes at full speed to get there in our boat. Titi had a new engine on her boat and was running it in. You have to gradually ease a new engine into service, not push it to its limits straight away. It was built in Czechoslovakia, so the instructions were in Czech, Polish and Russian. Our engine took just one hour to be run in; at half-speed. She thought that hers was thirty hours at the start setting. She is French, but the Czech, Polish and Russian instruction manual had been explained to her in Greek so she then retranslated it into English for us. We thought that there had been something lost in the translation.

The end result was that we just about reached these hallowed fishing grounds before dark. After a few demonstrations of how to carry out each manoeuvre and emergency briefings on every possible eventuality, we were each let loose with a set of fishing tackle. Henri was port side and I was starboard. It is not as easy as it looks. The particular fish we were after are bottom feeders and are caught by dropping a line with a weight attached to the seabed and baiting about five hooks, equally spaced 6 centimetres apart from the weight. You just hold the line between your fingers and you can tell if you have a fish attached, as the line vibrates as they try to remove the bait. At that point you give two sharp but short tugs and reel him in. I caught the first one after about half an hour. A skilled local would have had a bucketful by then. Next, Henri caught me and I caught Henri. First Henri would tug, declaring that she had the biggest of the species possible and could hardly reel it in. I then said that I also thought I had caught something huge. Titi, who was responsible for the oars and maintaining the boat geo-stationary, rushed over to help Henri. The two of them tugging together nearly had me over the side, and then it all became apparent. We eventually untangled the two weights, two lines and ten hooks, only to find that before catching each other, we had been very kindly feeding the fish without realizing it, and most of our bait was gone.

The best bait for this fish is 'their own kind', and a debate then ensued as to whether I should donate my catch to the cause. I pointed out that women had only been allowed to vote for relatively few years and therefore my decision held more sway that the two ladies put together. I already had great plans for my one-gramme whopper. I'd mentally put together a sauce, decided on the garnish and selected a nice Chablis to go with it. I'd glossed over the problems of getting a decent Chablis on the island, but if I could catch a fish, anything was possible that day. They were still insistent that I should have him executed on the spot and fed to his family and friends, based on what I saw as a very long shot for a repeat performance. Anyway, my wobbling bottom lip and hangdog expression won the day. Fred went back into the bucket and we continued with limited resources. Then a miracle struck: I caught another one. Titi insisted that no time should be lost, when they start to bite you have to strike when the iron is hot and get the hooks straight back in to catch more. Unlike with my first fish, I was allowed to extract the hook from this one unaided. In my eagerness to get back to the game, I squeezed Fred II a little too hard trying to get out the hook and managed to remove hook and gut him all at the same time. This technique is not to be recommended, but if it happens it is best to make sure that it isn't your own boat. Now it was Henri's turn to get the wobbly bottom lip. Nothing to do with the dismembered fish, but rather she wanted to catch one of her own. Fifteen minutes later she had one. It was bigger that my two put together; thank God for that! Now we could go home and prepare the sauce. Actually we had them fried with a little lemon juice and fresh Greek salad. No Chablis though; shame really.

We returned to the chandlers in Katapola to purchase the fishing tackle we required to continue our good fortune. We were a little apprehensive after our last visit, when our shopping trip involved most of the community and ended up with us buying enough kit to anchor the QEII. It was our lucky day. The manager for the day had attended Newcastle University, spoke good English despite the Geordie accent, and was a professional fisherman. All the kit we selected from the shelves ourselves was thrown back, just like a fish.

We were provided with the ideal line, the ideal weight and the ideal hooks for the job. We left the shop fully kitted for our first solo fishing trip.

Chapter IX Donkeys and Goats

The first week of June we only had one client and we took her down to Megali Glifada. She was amused to see a modern day young goatherd, Stamatis, sporting bright, sky blue overalls and sitting on his donkey, using binoculars to spot his charges and a mobile phone to contact his numerous girlfriends. Throughout the day he kept popping up unexpectedly from all directions. Firstly he'd be behind us and then in front, then he'd appear high on a mountain side to the left and then to the right. There are only three possible explanations to these seemingly impossible manoeuvres, firstly it was a family of identical quadruplets minding the goats, secondly, he had an underground tunnel system which would do a Vietcong goat herd proud, or lastly he moved like stealth greased weasel doings. His chosen colour scheme meant that he stood out like a sore thumb against the green and brown of the mountainside, but as soon as he stood on the skyline he took on the appearance of a bodiless man with his head just floating across the horizon. On our return from Glifada, a comment was made about the lack of goatherd sightings for an hour or so. The consensus of opinion was that we were probably under observation even as we spoke. Literally five seconds later, a head popped over a wall by Nikitas' old house and we were invited into the courtyard. Knowing the generosity of the islanders, we assumed it was an invitation for a coffee. It was in fact an invitation to witness the killing, skinning and disembowelling of a goat. Two unfortunate carcasses were already hanging in the house and a third was being dealt with. We had just missed the killing, saw a few minutes of the skinning, but remembered a pressing engagement that precluded us from staying for the third act. A real shame, but, 'perhaps another time', we assured him. The answer to the goatherd's gymnastic abilities became apparent when we met him later in the day at the hotel. He was now dressed in civvies and was introduced as Nikitas' nephew.

We experienced more facts of animal life with another group later in June. On our way through Asphondilitis, the most remote farming community on the island, we met the butcher Stephanas from Ormos, coming along on his donkey complete with the inevitable mobile phone; the butcher not the donkey. Stephanas is a slightly rotund red-faced gentleman in his mid-fifties with thinning hair. We were the first people he had met on his one and a half hour ride and so he stopped for a chat. He was picking up some meat from the community to sell to the restaurants in Ormos. There was to be a very large group of Greeks from Crete arriving on the island on the Saturday for a holiday weekend. The demand for food was very high, which is why it was a particularly dangerous time for goats, calves, fish, chickens or generally anything that can't answer back or run fast enough. The butcher had the reputation for being the only one in Greece who you have to make an appointment to see, thus the mobile phone.

The procedure being that at the appointed time you went along, discussed your requirements, negotiated the cost and placed the order. He then went out and did a bit of killing and your order was delivered to your door. It was never quite what you ordered; it might be goat instead of chicken or beef instead of lamb. It wasn't his fault if whatever was particularly slow on its feet that day wasn't precisely what was written in the order book, but it was always pretty close; it was meat.

After spending an hour or so on the beach at Halara on the other side of the island, we made our way back down to Ormos. As we approached the village coming down the still used donkey tracks through Potamos, we heard quite a commotion closing in on us from behind. There was wailing and shouting and snorting, then we saw two enormous bulls heading our way at a rate of knots. After a very short discussion and a skills and abilities audit, we discovered that none of us were qualified matadors and the group decision was to adopt a cowardly approach to the problem. We dived into the courtyard of a house under renovation and let events unfold on the outside without our participation. The first animal to pass was a very large cow being led on a long rope by the butcher's assistant, and following were the two bulls who were more interested in the cow than their reason for this afternoon saunter. We wondered if they were allowed a last request! Behind them came our friend the butcher, leading his donkey, to which were strapped six writhing and bleating goats. At least all the meat stayed fresh on its journey. Who needs refrigerated lorries anyway?

We were having terrible trouble with crickets at the house. They were becoming a real problem. They were eating everything in sight and one even took a lump out of Henri's shoulder one morning. They were getting everywhere and so big that they left a horrible mess when you stamped on them and their droppings were the size of those of a mouse. We were killing and disposing of two large shovelfuls a day. The technique had been named cricket-croquet and involved clobbering the little bastards with a brush and batting them into a corner to be shovelled. One even got into our printer and came out sitting on a page with a huge grin on his face. I soon wiped that off for him.

One day in July, just before the 'Cretan Invasion', we were seeing our clients onto the ferry and witnessed the chaotic loading of freight. Some of the lorries seemed to be very precariously loaded. We were told that on one occasion, a lorry was so overloaded and leaning dangerously that the captain demanded to speak to the driver. The driver assured him that it would be fine and that his friend in Athens would take it off the ferry. The captain told him that the only condition under which he would accept this dangerous and overloaded vehicle was if the driver travelled with it, so that if there was a problem he could sort out the mess. The driver reluctantly agreed and the ferry sailed. Just as the boat turned away from the quay, the captain noticed a familiar figure on the quay furtively hiding behind the harbour light pillar. The boat pulled back into the port and the lorry was offloaded.

Chapter X The Cretan Invasion

Holiday weekend arrived. The island was at fever pitch, awaiting the invasion of Cretans for the bank holiday weekend. They were from one of Greece's largest shipping lines and consisted of employees, family and friends. They were bringing in one of their own ships and it was one of the biggest ever to come to the island. The whole operation was of considerable commercial interest to all the islanders. The population of the island is only 1,800 and the road had only been finished a few years previously, resulting in a limited number of people having cars. Fifteen hundred visitors were expected and over five hundred cars. As mentioned earlier, every fattened calf and goat had been slaughtered, but this did not solve the accommodation problem. Grannies had been thrown out of their beds and put in with the goats. Children had been persuaded that this was the weekend to experience camping. Donkeys had been thrown out of stables, which had been whitewashed inside and out, and notices hung promoting Amorgos as the next best place to stay after Bethlehem. Extra police had been drafted in from Athens, in case anyone should start to make a fuss about the star rating of their stable.

Our policeman had to dig out his uniform. It was a pity he couldn't find his own hat and had to borrow one from a considerably smaller colleague. The seconded police were paraded around the village all day and briefed on potential hot spots and the local strategy for riot control. They seemed to spend a considerable time in most tavernas and got more 'confused', but happily content as the day progressed.

Then there was a crisis. Just a few hours before the invasion of the honoured guests, a couple were spotted sunbathing nude on the main beach in the port of Aegiali. We couldn't risk offending any visiting prudes from Crete. An emergency like this would usually warrant the use of the island police car. Unfortunately this particular marvel of modern automobile engineering, which made Del Boy's van look like a souped-up Ferrari, was last seen on the servicing ramp at the island garage, decidedly short of a few crucial parts. A one-seater moped was requisitioned and the 'chief of police' demanded to be driven to the scene of the crime. Two very large policemen on a very small moped doing twenty five kilometres per hour flat out to this emergency would be almost acceptable going past once, but when said nudists got wind of the impending raid and covered up, the search took quite a number of passes. When it was obvious that the crime figures of the island were not going to be improved upon this month, remaining as always at nil, the search was discontinued and the traffic control plan was put into action as the influx of cars was awaited.

The ship was too large to dock in Ormos Aegialis, so everyone had to drive across from the other port, Katapola, which was 22 kilometres away. Was it all going to be a damp squid, were the numbers exaggerated, was it all just a big rumour put about so the local policeman could have some colleagues over from Athens to play? It started like the hum of a bee and then the hum of a few bees and then a swarm of bees and then they came over the mountain like the biggest caterpillar in the world. Hundreds of cars, all descending on the village, red ones, blue ones, big ones, small ones. They choked up the road, and brought the port to a standstill. These visitors complained because they thought that they had come to a small and quiet idyllic island and to them it looked like central Athens, cars were everywhere, we had the biggest traffic jam in the world and no one knew where to go. The village elders sat in front of their favourite cafeneions, resting their chins on their hands crossed on top of their sticks, watching the whole pantomime unfold with the usual laid back and contented attitude to life. They knew it would all sort itself out in the end, and there was absolutely no point in getting excited about anything. They were right, the police had it all in hand. A roadblock was set up at the entrance to the village and drivers were given directions to their final accommodation. The only problem was that none of the seconded police knew the island and were still a little confused from their afternoon walk about. The local bus driver and the grocer were sent for and used as geographic consultants, the traffic started flowing again, well just up to the point where the village was full and they had to park back along the road and out into the sea almost as far back as Crete!

Chapter XI Tavernas and Shops

We had a few days off between groups in the summer and decided one day to support local commerce and cement Anglo-Greek relations by touring the few tavernas in the port. Early afternoon is a good time for this exercise, as all the family is usually there supported by a number of staff. It was early in the high season, so they were just training up new waiters in preparation for the start of the short busy season. The first establishment we came to was closed and the taverna sign removed. Now we usually get enough intelligence fed to us on the island jungle telegraph to know when places are changing hands or closing down, but we had no such information on this particular restaurant. Nothing was more surprising than to find the same situation at the second one. Had a plague struck? We checked ourselves for spots or other telltale signs. Up until the last century, there had been a leper colony on the small but now uninhabited island of Nikouria, across from our house. Perhaps leprosy had returned to the island? We checked the security of our arms and legs and with relief found them securely attached. With great joy we found the third taverna open and it seemed to be business as usual. It is called To Limani, which means, 'The Harbour'. This is the main taverna in the village and is the most popular with tourists and islanders alike. It is family run and they have quite a number of staff to help out in the summer months. The grandfather, Andonis, always sat outside as a permanent feature and was readily available as the village oracle on any subject from the totally unpredictable ferry schedule to the equally unpredictable weather, from the results of the forthcoming elections to the number of Germans likely to invade the island this summer. The longevity of the islanders results from their relaxed and laid back life style, helped considerably by their diet of fresh fruit, vegetables, fish and olive oil. Many therefore still remember the German occupation and still hold a grudge. Many years ago an unsuspecting tourist arrived on a black motorbike and side car. He got stones thrown at him by a little old lady who thought that the Nazis had returned. At the taverna the grandmother, Katina, paraded her grandchild backwards and forwards along the front in a three-pronged strategy. Firstly to keep the child quiet and out of his parents' way whilst they worked. Secondly, it gave everyone the chance to tell the doting grandmother what a wonderful grandchild she had, but thirdly and most importantly it allowed her to keep an eye on the overall operation. It is very much a matriarchal society and she was in charge. It was she who did all the negotiating with suppliers, the accounts, pricings and administration. It is her name that appears on all business cards and letterheads, even to this day, although unfortunately this wonderful couple, Katina and Andonis, are no longer with us. Their sons Paniotis and Theo are now in charge with their respective wives. Everyone still refers to the restaurant as Katina's and indeed this name still appears on the sign.

That day there was no grandfather outside to seek opinions from, no child walking taking place and no sign of any waiters. Now in desperate need of a cold beer, we risked the wrath of Katina and uninvited, we entered the hallowed ground of her kitchen. There she was at the cooker?! Andonis was bashing spuds and the younger members of the family were practicing the finer art of balancing five plates and six bottles on a tray whose design features are more conducive to carrying one ouzo. We helped ourselves to a beer from the fridge with the approving nod of a very harassed looking management waiter and took a seat amongst a few even more harassed looking tourists who were still quite clearly waiting for breakfast at 14.00 in the afternoon. During a lull in the activity, we discretely asked of the nature of the plague that had quite clearly struck down the majority of the taverna owners and staff. It turned out to be called 'The Taxman'. Every year the taxman from Naxos makes a surprise inspection to check that the correct taxes are being paid for businesses run and staff employed. Every year everything is found to be completely in order because there are only a couple of tavernas and they are totally manned by the families involved. He knows there used to be many more establishments and enhanced staff in those remaining, but now most are closed and the others cannot afford staff. He assumes that the recent downturn in business and the hardship suffered by the owners is the result of an inexplicable decline in tourism. He didn't in fact notice that this phenomenon exactly coincided with improved telecommunications between the harbour-front taverna owners in Naxos and their colleagues in Amorgos. As soon as the taxman gets on the ferry, the call goes out and the islanders have five hours to prepare for this 'no-notice' inspection. It must be said that most of these establishments try to arrange papers for their summer staff. However, the administration takes so long that by the time the papers come through the season is over.

The old days were quite a worry for the shop and taverna owners, especially with the compulsory introduction of cash registers. If the machine breaks down, it can take weeks to send it back to Athens for repair or replacement. During this time everything has to be done manually and the Greek regulations for business ownership makes Queen's Regulations in the military look like the guidelines for running a Brownie troop. One, fortunately punctilious, restaurant owner had a major cash register malfunction in the middle of a very busy lunch period. There was paper everywhere, tempers were frayed and a particularly difficult couple who seemed to be extremely over dressed for the occasion were insisting on a receipt. A manual one was produced with abject apologies for the format and the reason explained. It really was his lucky day; not only did he pass this taxman's spot inspection with flying colours, but there was nothing that the over-dressed couple didn't know about the internal workings of the dreaded cash machine. It was fixed within minutes instead of weeks and they were on their way, smiles all round. The short delay in their departure, whilst fixing the machine, presumably also gave time to activate the island jungle telegraph, and by the end of the day, the whole island was in the taxman's good books. Quite a few ouzos were drunk that evening and they certainly didn't go through the books.

One day Maria, a lady from the village, lovingly prepared her husband his lunch of veal and zucchini casserole. She has never been renowned for her cooking but Stephanas, the butcher, assured her that this was the very best meat money could buy and she really could not go wrong with its preparation. At 15.00 in the afternoon we observed her storming through the village in the direction of the butcher's shop with an enormous steaming pot of casserole. The butcher is of course only available by appointment and was probably busy stalking some unsuspecting prey in the mountains out of mobile phone coverage. The casserole was therefore left with his neighbour with instructions to give it to Stephanas on his return. Initially it was assumed that this was part of some sort of bartering deal or just a very kind gesture. Then it transpired that her husband found his lunch very bitter and would not eat it. It couldn't possibly be her cooking that was at fault, it therefore had to be the meat and so she was returning it for a refund or replacement. As soon as she had stormed off, presumably to now tackle a slightly less culinary challenging feat such as bread and cheese, the now gathered group of neutral observers decided to sample said dish. The unanimous decision was that the meat was excellent, but the sauce and vegetable preparation were decidedly suspect. We waited as long as we could for the butcher's return to find out the corollary to the saga, but had to leave before he returned from what must have been a particularly long hunt for supplies. Busy with clients the following day, we had to wait impatiently until that evening for the outcome. Apparently upon his return Stephanas and his assistant were in agreement with the by then not inconsiderably sized committee and had the meat for their lunch. In the interests of marital relations he provided Maria with different produce free of charge and kept his fingers crossed that she would have greater success in its preparation.

Vangelis from Celini had not been well for some time. It was late summer and getting towards the end of the short tourist season. He was tired and run down. Amongst many other things he had developed a rash on his arms. He is allergic to everything and was on so many pills he was rattling like the grocer's truck. Early one morning, Vangelis made the mistake of going to see the grocer, Agiris, whilst the local doctor Socrates was there. 'Ti kaneis?' Agiris asked Vangelis ('how are you?'). Before Vangelis could utter a word, Socrates answered for him, immediately diagnosing his condition. (Well, I suppose the doctor was better qualified to answer.)

A debate ensued between the doctor the grocer and those present as to the best course of action for Vangelis' condition. He had gone in for a number of items, but managed to escape with just a loaf of bread before the subject of euthanasia was raised.

A little later that morning we went to see Agiris just to buy some bread and eggs, yet another shopping adventure.

There were six other people in the shop waiting to be served, all visitors to the island. As we entered they were ignored as if they didn't exist. We were welcomed like long lost friends and 'Raki, raki?' was shouted at us as if it was some sort of informal greeting rather than rocket fuel. This locally produced clear liquor is about nine hundred percent proof and certainly not to be taken internally. Agiris had just taken delivery of a very large keg of the stuff, which can be bought loose if you bring along your own bottle. It is recommended to use a bottle that has been made for ICI to transport sulphuric acid. The grocer's wife managed their other shop in the next village and Agiris used this guaranteed freedom from discovery to hold parties inside and outside his shop with this keg of raki as a source of leglessness and blurred vision. As the controller of supplies and as the FD, MD and chairman of the operation all rolled into one, his wife, Maria, without doubt would have well and truly killed him if she knew what was going on. On that day, what looked like a British Rail plastic beaker was produced and half-filled with the liquor. The tourists looked on, contemplating the commercial opportunities for opening a drying out clinic on the island, as I set to with the rocket fuel, my Greek improving considerably with every mouthful. Whilst I was trying to keep on an even keel and focus on the cup, Henri selected a loaf from the top of the breadbasket on the counter. It was ceremoniously whipped from her hand and Agiris disappeared, head first, into a huge sack behind the counter and reappeared proffering an identical loaf. He thrust his index finger deep into the centre of it to demonstrate the freshness of said item and the offending original was replaced in the basket for the next unsuspecting foreigner. Trays of eggs were prominent on the counter but when 'avga' were requested, yet another disappearing act was called for as he delved deep into a large fridge at the back of the shop.

'These were laid this morning by my chickens and are the best on the island', we were told. The problem with most local produce is that some is not available on the open market, they are all part of the island wide barter system. No tally is kept as to who owes who, you just give people what you can or help out when you can, the theory being that it all balances out in the end. Thus there was no charge for the eggs. We left the shop with slightly blurred vision, half a dozen eggs and one loaf resembling an enormous doughnut, all for the price of the bread.

Later in the year we took our clients to Theologos again. It is the fourth-century monastery where we attended the earlier festival in the spring and one and a half hour's walk from the nearest village. Inside are some incredibly well preserved frescos from the period and the monks have lovingly maintained the whole building over the times. It is without doubt one of the most spectacular buildings on the island and rarely visited by tourists due to its location. A little further around the mountain is a now derelict house. This is where an old goatherd and farmer Tubuckarris used to live. When Tubuck used to live there about forty years ago, he was half a day's donkey ride away from the nearest cigarette supply, and like most islanders had an insatiable desire for the weed. He used to overcome the problem by growing his own tobacco on the terraces. As much as he tried however, he couldn't replicate cigarette paper. At one of the twice-yearly festivals at the monastery he was pondering his predicament during a very involved and protracted sermon by the priest. Idly thumbing and flicking the pages of the delicate pages of the ancient handwritten prayer book, it came to him like a vision from God. It was clearly meant to be! The paper was the perfect weight and texture to 'roll your own' and he was sure that the ornate and intricate calligraphy would not affect the taste. Frequent nightly sorties were made and supplies acquired. History does not record if the demise of Tubuck coincided with the total depletion of all the pages of all the ancient prayer books, but there are certainly none to be seen today.

Chapter XII The 'Skop' Again

In order to make sure that our clients would have no problems with a transfer and hotel in Naxos, we went with them one day on the new 'Express' Skopelitis. The lack of ferry services that year meant that they would lose a day on Amorgos, but get a chance to look around Naxos for the evening. The new boat had an impressive passenger lounge and, apart from a few locals, we had it all to ourselves, with the tourists preferring to stay on deck gathering the last rays of sunshine before returning to rain swept England or France. To this day, this boat is the lifeline that connects the few islands between here and Naxos and usually calls in at Donousa, Koufinisi, Schinousa, Iraklia and then Naxos. It returns to the same islands after a three-hour stay in Naxos, which enables people to go and see any officials such as the dreaded taxman, the bank manager or solicitor. Packages are put on at various islands and picked up by the recipients at their respective destinations. That morning the grocer was on the quay to put on supplies for some of the smaller islands, and the doctor was also meeting the boat. We have no idea why, but the doctor always seemed to be meeting every boat that came in, perhaps he was just desperately looking for trade. The policeman came with us to spend the day on Donousa, presumably to ensure law was still in order there, as they don't have their own 'police force'. The journey out was uneventful. We dropped the policeman off first, but not before he'd had a large scotch on board (presumably to steady his nerves to face the vagaries of this tiny island). A few tourists came and went at other islands, and some goods changed hands. As the 5-hour trip progressed, the sea got rougher and rougher. By the time we got to Naxos it was very rough. We settled our clients down in their hotel, the most charming on the island. It is set against the city wall in the narrow streets of the old Venetian sector and furnished in period style.

We then did a little bit of business involving Greek negotiation tactics, which are always lengthy and sometimes extremely noisy, and returned to the ferry completely washed out. The tourists were starting to arrive on the islands and the decks were pretty full, but again the lounge was quiet. The steward was busy putting out carrier bags everywhere as makeshift sick bags, and he made sure that the few tourists down below each had one to hand. We felt honoured that we were treated like the locals and not offered one. It was a good job we had taken the jolly old pills though, because to say it was rough would be an understatement. The ferry is based on Amorgos in Katapola, so it had to get back, but it really was on the limits for it. The movement of the boat was different on every sector between the various islands, depending if it was going with, against or across the swell, or a combination of all three. The bow was digging deep into the waves and mountains of seawater were being thrown up to either side as the passengers threw up over the side. It was almost impossible to walk about and most of the passengers were too ill to do so anyway. They stoically stayed on deck soaking wet and extremely green. We picked up our chief priest, Papa Spirithon, at Iraklia, and looking at some of the passengers he probably thought his services might very well be needed. Then at every stop he got off to greet and talk to his flock on the quay. On more than one occasion the wind nearly took off his low 'travelling' hat. Papa Spirithon is a very large character with obligatory beard and long hair tied back under his tall priest's hat. He is jovial to the extreme and can be heard from one village to the other with his loud booming voice. Each stop on the return took an inordinate amount of time, due to the amount of stores to be off-loaded which had come initially from Athens on a larger ship. At some ports the ferry was rolling so violently that first the left-hand side of the stern ramp was one metre off the quay, and then it slammed down, allowing the right-hand side to have a turn at this manoeuvre. This was all quite a challenging movement to work with whilst unloading goods. At Koufinisi, two pallet loads of tiles had to be off-loaded, but the forklift truck from the island was only large enough to lift a couple of boxes of lemons. This was solved by three large men hanging on the back of it to counterbalance the weight of the tiles on the front, all precariously managed on a ramp swaying between plus twenty and minus twenty degrees. Usually this type of spectacle is watched by a mass of bemused tourists all straining to get a view of the free pantomime. On this occasion I had no need to fight through hoards of fat Germans or complaining Frogs, as they were all sitting down very quietly contemplating the lack of content in their stomachs. We picked up the policeman at Donousa after his day of inspection, wondering if he had ever got past the bar on the quay where he was sitting when we came alongside. He spent the next hour in a heated discussion with Papa Spirithon which involved a lot of finger wagging and poking from both sides. One could only surmise the subjects involved. We are frequently involved in arguments with Papa Spirithon about roads to his monasteries. He wants them to make his life easier. We tell him that whilst he has a donkey to ride (poor thing), we have to walk and we enjoy the paths as they are. This always progresses to him asking us what we will do when we are too old to walk. We say in unison, 'we will get donkeys'. He then says, 'what will you do when you are too old to ride a donkey?' Again in unison we say, 'we will get a helicopter'. This usually terminates the argument. In all, the return journey took six hours, and for the final sector we went up on deck and stepped over a few prone bodies to go to the flying bridge to watch the sunset over Naxos. It was quite spectacular, although no one else on deck seemed to be interested. We then went back inside and, just so the policeman didn't feel bad about drinking alone, we ordered more beer. Sitting opposite was an English couple, two of the very few tourists inside. All I did was to quaff half the can in one large gulp and declare it great and the British man made yet another very weavy dash for the gents. They really don't make British tourists like they used to.

Towards the end of the season we thanked Vasilis, the Arab boy in Celini, for serving our beer, only to be told by him in no uncertain terms, 'my name is not Vasilis, it is Basili'. It turns out that Vasilis/Basili had revolted and would not accept the Greek name that had apparently been thrust upon him. It seemed that his employer, Vangelis, didn't want to be seen to be employing foreign labour when there were locals looking for seasonal work. The theory being that if he was called a Greek name, everyone would be fooled into thinking that this little Arab boy, who would look far more in place on the back of a camel rather than a donkey, was in fact born and bred on the island. He was taken aside, and as voices were raised, an argument ensued in a mixture of Arabic, English and Greek. As this was taking place in the open kitchen, we left before knives started to fly. The following morning we found out that the boy had been frog-marched into the village ferry office and a one-way ticket to Athens was being negotiated when he succumbed and agreed to toe the party line. We asked by what name we should now call him and were informed that he would now answer to anything!

Basili went in the end. He was allowed to borrow his boss's motorbike to go into the village (200 metres), the petrol station (300 metres), or if there was an absolute supply crisis, he could go as far as the next village, as long as he had a police escort. One Saturday night he and his little boyfriend decided they would go out for a night on the town, and both piled onto this single seater to take it to the capital of the island 12 kilometres away. Although a challenge, with two on a very small bike around many hairpin bends up in the mountains, this would have been just about feasible if the bike had any lights at all and better brakes. Given a full moon and tougher shoes for braking, it may also have been just about possible. But there was no moon and they were in sandals which were more suitable for riding a camel. They made it about five hundred metres outside the village before coming off the road. The following day Basili, covered from head to foot in plasters and bandages, managed to recover the bike. It still worked, just, but would only go around in circles when the handlebars were central. This would have restricted his operating radius if he still had the job. Unfortunately he didn't take the resultant disciplinary pep talk from Vangelis too well and threw a little Arabic tantrum. This resulted in a beer glass being thrown back into the washing-up bowl, and the subsequent retrieval left the boss with a very badly gashed hand. Vangelis was rushed to the doctor, who is always desperate for trade, but on this occasion he was out. He missed a God-sent opportunity to wield a needle and thread and practice his cross-stitch on Vangelis' hand. There were copious Arabic tears and even more copious Greek blood all over the place. After that incident, Vangelis changed his job spec as follows: 'Young Greek speaking girl required preferably with waitressing experience, must have a Greek name and good night vision. Taxmen's daughters need not apply'.

We inherited the dizziest client money can buy. On day one of the programme we were all waiting for her, wearing suitable gear for a mountain walk: shorts, tee shirts and sunhats. Victoria came down from her room sans hat as she wished to purchase one on the island that would 'get her into the mood of Amorgos'. The village's two grocery shops are not renowned for their millinery departments. Potatoes, candles, raki and even a scrubbing brush, but definitely not hats. Fortunately for her, a small boutique run by our friend Christina, a Swedish lady, had just opened and they did have a small number of hats, all imported from Thailand. Well, it would get her into an island mood even if it wasn't quite the right geographic location or culture. We just hoped she didn't buy the little finger cymbals to go with it, as this could cause havoc on hotel Greek nights. On day two Victoria appeared, eventually, sporting a long and flowing flowery dress and an extremely large and ornate straw hat complete with bow. She would have looked entirely in place in the Royal Enclosure at Royal Ascot, had it not been for the hiking boots sticking out from under the hem of her dress. Our first port of call was the monastery of Hozoviotissa. This involves walking up 267 steps from the car park. She made it up the steps and back down again and then announced that she was far too hot to continue that day and she thought that instead she should go shopping for a lighter hat. In actual fact, all she would have needed to do was to buy a mobile air conditioning unit and position it under the boater, there would still have been plenty of room to spare for a picnic lunch and a bottle of wine. For the rest of the week, she wore much more sensible apparel and a small and cool sun hat. She had decided to stay on for a few extra days after our other clients had left and asked us to book her into the hotel for these extra nights. After we returned from another exciting boat ride on the Express Skopelitis, Victoria had disappeared without paying her bill or leaving any message for us. It is a small island however and we traced her within a few minutes to a hotel on the beach. She returned the following day and paid her bill. She didn't make any attempt to tell us of her move, but we went to see her the following day to arrange her transfer and ferry tickets that are all part the package we offer. We found that she had disappeared without paying, again, and this time also without trace. They went to clean her room in the morning and found her to be missing. All her luggage, belongings and personal effects were gone. All that remained was a large straw hat, with bow, hanging on a hook on the wall. That night, there was a strange campfire burning in the old leper colony on the deserted island of Nikouria across the water from our house. We wondered if Basili and Victoria were setting up home together over there, they certainly deserved each other.

If our previous presumptions were right, this whirlwind romance was very short lived. Basili returned with his tail between his legs, begging for his old job back and the accommodation that went with it. Previously he had progressed to the dizzy heights of waiter, this was however a restricted licence to practice with certain limitations applied. No handling of cash, no taking orders, certainly no wine waiting and only removing caps from beer bottles under strict supervision. Now he had to start again from the bottom and earn the respect and trust that promotion brings. He went back onto chair painting duties.

There was no news of Victoria, but we found out that she had left some money with another hotel guest to pay her bills. She was certainly strange, but obviously not dishonest. This is good, as the former fits in well on Amorgos, but certainly not the latter. She was obviously enamoured with the island as she has been back a number of times since, independently and much more level headed.

Basili eventually left again and that time forever. When you hold the lowest position in an organization, it is a major HR problem for the Chairman or MD to demote you after you burn down half his house. He therefore had to go. Basili and his little boyfriend, who was also an Arab, decided that it would be all very romantic to go to sleep by candlelight. There was a draft in the room, so they needed to find a sheltered spot. Set into the wall is the electricity meter and fuse box with a very nice clear plastic door. With some excellent lateral thinking, assisted considerably by enormous amounts of alcohol, it seemed to them to make an ideal fitted lantern with draft free door. The inevitable happened, and it was only by a miracle that they got out alive. They decided to try to get everything rectified without telling Vangelis. He thought they had been very quiet for two days and working particularly well, but they were receiving mysterious phone calls and disappearing for long periods during the working day. Although Vangelis didn't live in this house, he did use it for showers sometimes. It was only a matter of time before the urge for a nice hot shower came over him. He thought that he had better check with the boys about the state of the house, to make sure there were no full ashtrays or empty beer cans around, and to give them a chance to clear it up before he saw it, because they knew how house proud he was. He certainly didn't expect the reaction he got to this enquiry. Panic ensued, Basili tried to hide under the kitchen butcher's block and crouched like Arabs do, shaking with his hands covering his head and assuming that if he couldn't see anyone no one could see him. His friend, who was a little older, considered the honest and open approach to be the best way. He was sure that Vangelis would understand and not lose his temper with them. He didn't and he did. It also set the owner's skin complaint back at least a month as the doctor had told him it is caused by stress and he really should try to remain calm.

Chapter XIII Post

We received a letter from my parents, who were on holiday in France. Post is a big problem on Amorgos if you live anywhere where the postman, Dimitris, cannot drive right up to your door in his little van. This applies to most people on the island. When we arrived, Dimitris was in his late forties, short and a little rotund with ruddy features, and he always had a smile on his face. He did a short round, walking from his van around the centre of some villages, but two fields away from a cart track and six kilometres from a village, we did not stand an earthly. In this case you could either pick your post up at the post office that was open three mornings a week for six weeks of the year, or nominate a friend to receive your mail and arrange to collect from them. By the time UK mail had been sorted in England, flown to Athens and sorted again, shipped to Naxos and sorted again, it then goes on the Skopelitis to Amorgos. As we know, this only ran a few times a week and not at all if it was rough. Dimitris then would then pick the Aegiali bag up from the other port and brought it to his post office here, a drive of one hour, to sort it again for local delivery. Deliveries were only every three days. The whole process took nearly three weeks. Oh, and by the way, if you expected to retire to this island to absorb yourself in your passion for philately, forget it. Dimitris also collected stamps, and if he saw a good one when sorting, off it came. He did however always apologise for the hole in the envelope or card. He was such a charming and cheerful postman that no one really minded. It was bit late by then anyway.

Many people here have property that they only occupy for six months of the year. If you live in some other part of Greece for the winter, it is no problem to pay bills and deal with administration such as electricity bills and election forms. If you reside outside Greece in the winter, as many people do, it is more of a problem. The better-organized people arrange for someone on the island to deal with this administration for them, whilst others face innumerable problems trying to pick up the pieces in the spring. One year, our friend Christina returned from her winter buying trip to the Far East for her boutique in the village and realized to her horror that she had forgotten to pay the electricity bill. She was quite astounded when she discovered that the electric company hadn't cut off the supply. They will do this under such circumstances without hesitation. This would have presented her with enormous problems with the business and substantial extra charges for reconnection. The next day she saw Dimitris, and after getting her up to date with island life, he mentioned her electricity bill. She said that she would take it and pay it straight away and said how lucky she had been in not being cut off. 'Don't worry', he said, 'pay me when you've got time. When I saw your bill a few months ago, I knew that you wouldn't be back in time to pay it and would be cut off, so I opened it and paid it for you'. Now that's what you call service.

Unfortunately, for personal reasons, Dimitris had to leave the island at short notice to live on the main land. There he became the chauffeur for His Beatitude Christodoulos Archbishop of Athens and All Greece. This did somewhat curtail his philately. However, it gave him plenty of spare time, whilst waiting in the car for His Beatitude, to collate his collection. A few years later, after the Archbishop died, Dimitris returned to the island. It is really nice to see his cheerful smiling face back on Amorgos.

His departure, however, left us with no post office at all and no postman. Fortunately, Anna, the owner of the newsagents and cigarette shop, volunteered to fulfill the role. It was a job her mother used to do, so she had some experience with it. The problem was that she didn't want to lose her shop by moving to the post office. The post office was closed, a table was placed in the corner of the shop and a sub-post office was born. Eventually a post office sign went up outside and then there was even a counter. It was smaller than the table, but there were postal sorting slots behind it. A few years later a proper little post office was built above the shop. Anna still does rounds once a week to each of the three villages, but we collect from the shop known to us as 'fags and mags' due to their wares. As there are only three permanent residents of Stroumbos, where we now live, our post is left on the side in 'fags and mags'. This is very convenient as we can collect post even when the post office is closed due to postal rounds. Anna is supported in running the shop by her husband Lefteris, her mother and an elderly uncle. They are a delightful and very extended family. Her husband is usually involved in other tasks away from the shop, so the running of it is left to the elderly lady and gentleman. They will sell stamps, but that is where the service stops. If you have something more than a letter to send, you just leave it on the counter unstamped. Anna sends it to the island's main post office the following day and you pay the next time you see her. If there is a recorded delivery letter, you take it and sign for it the next time you see her. This may not necessarily be at fags and mags, it is more often in a taverna or shop in one of the villages. Considering four hundred people live at this end of the island, Anna has an incredible memory. She will greet us in the street and tell us that there is post for us in the shop.

We went to collect our post one day and Anna was giggling away and laying all the letters on the road outside the Post Office. We thought that this was a rather bizarre practice, but you get used to most things on Amorgos. When we got closer we noticed that all the letters and parcels were soaking wet. She was putting them in the sun to dry. We said 'what happened? Have you had a plumbing leak in the shop?' 'No' she said, 'they were throwing the mail sacks off the ship onto the quay and this one missed and went into the sea'. The only mail for us was an annual return for Companies House in the UK. I filed a very wrinkled return with a letter of explanation and heard no further about it. I am sure that one went in their book of company's excuses.

Vangelis' dog, Daego, died. He had been ill with cancer for some time and it was a relief when he died. There was no practicing vet on the island at the time, so there was no means of putting an animal out of its misery; you just had to do the best you could. For his last twenty four hours he was spoon fed sleeping tablets with a little alcohol to help him sleep. Daego was a fine old gentleman of sixteen. He was one of the most enormous dogs of dubious and various breeds. He could be extremely gentle when he wanted to be, but would take no messing when he wanted to be awkward. He had laid siege to people's apartments in Athens and had the occupants pinned in corners afraid to move. On one occasion, Vangelis' brother and his wife, Aris and Gitty, wanted to use Vangelis' car to pick up some clients. Not many people on the island at that time had cars, so these commodities were particularly precious. The use of this actual car was of particular value that year, as it had spent nine months off the road the previous year under repair. No, it wasn't a major renovation or a complete body off re-spray operation, it was just a butterfly valve in the carburetor that was stuck. The garage here had spent some time trying to get a new valve from Athens, but could only obtain the whole unit. They then managed, somehow, to put it in back to front and also rewire the electrics on the distributor the wrong way round. The resultant blinding flash and bang rendered further parts of the car unserviceable. Again weeks and weeks of waiting produced various other spare parts from Athens. The more spare parts that were available increased the number of combinations of reconstructing said vehicle and resulted in yet further dismantling. After six months or so, half the engine was out and the garage floor was strewn with parts, old and new. No problem you may think, just consult the workshop manual. What manual? By this time no one could remember where each part had come from and in which order they went back. The car was pushed onto the ferry accompanied by boxes of bits and pieces and shipped to Athens for reconstruction. It was back in service exactly nine months after the very small problem it went in for in the first place.

So it can be seen that this car was particularly precious to them. The clients were also commercially important. Aris and Gitty, apart from being highly qualified academics, ran a herb business on the island. They picked herbs in the mountains, collecting them in accordance with the phases of the moon, and they also cultivated some of their own. These were then packaged up and sold with instructions for use: infuse and inhale, add to a sauce, put in with clothes, rub on 'listed' body parts, smoke (but only with police permission) etc.

Gitty also took people into the mountains for outdoor seminars on the subject. That year had been disastrous for them, due to the very dry spring. The herbs were over before they really got to their best. They picked relatively few and their seminars were very short lived. The clients that week were their first and amongst their last for the year. The valued car was desperately needed to meet these people. Daego had different ideas. In the early morning someone had let him out for a walk and he had jumped into the car. His hips were particularly bad and he had landed badly, trapping himself between the front and back seats. He couldn't get out on his own and the only person who could possibly extract him, Vangelis, was in bed after working an extremely long night and no one was exactly sure which of his various houses he was in. Daego couldn't drive and no one was prepared to get closer than about two metres to this snarling, snapping monster, and so the car went nowhere. To say there was a heated discussion when Vangelis arrived at lunchtime is an understatement. Nice one, Daego.

Chapter XIV Chora

Sometimes it is nice just to have a couple to show around instead of a large group. One couple in our first year were enormous fun. They have been back now two more times, so we must be doing something right. People do seem to be happy following us around the mountains. However, it may be similar to the case of an officer, of whom on his annual report his commanding officer said, 'His men will follow him anywhere, if only out of curiosity'. They were the first really serious walkers we had and we were just whizzing around the mountains, and they bought us beer! We completed the monastery walk following the old donkey path from Aegiali to Chora in just four-and-a-half hours. That was the longest walk in our programme. It took our first clients seven hours!

Chora is an interesting little 'city' with a Venetian castle, a church on every street corner, little winding stone paved streets, an archaeological collection and a fascinating underground Byzantine aqueduct in the old quarter. This cistern, called Kato Lakkos, is mentioned in a guidebook, but impossible to find. Some years ago we knew we were very close to it, but not close enough. We kidnapped a little old man, refusing to release him until he took us there. 'Take us to your Byzantine aqueduct' doesn't have quite the same ring as 'take us to your leader', and I suppose we were lucky that he didn't take us to the police; but it worked. After winding around the old and dilapidated streets and ruined houses of outer Chora, you drop down some steps to an old wooden door. Upon opening it, you go down some very steep and seriously dodgy stone steps into an amazing series of vaults. It is always pleasantly cool down there and you can only hear the dripping of the water into the large underground lake. When your eyes get used to the dim light, you can see the cool, clear water, and above are large arches showing a Venetian influence. It was built in medieval times and corresponded with the first organized occupation of Chora, and in the fifteenth century the Venetians renovated it. It has remained untouched ever since.

The archaeological collection in Chora contains some very interesting finds from all over the island. The circumstances in which some of these exhibits have come to light is sometimes more fascinating than the items themselves. There is a fifth-century BC bust of a lady about the size of a large paperweight (and indeed if that is what it had been used for, it wouldn't be in the state is today). Instead of being stone coloured, it is dyed green. It was found in a lady's kitchen, where it had been used for generations to pound down, flatten and tenderise vine leaves before stuffing them. There is a two metre high statue of a man, again fifth-century BC, whose buttocks have been worn away. It was found when someone was renovating an old donkey stable and took out the doorstep. The underside of the step revealed the features of a man. This invaluable piece had been placed face down as the stable doorstep and this unfortunate individual's backside had been trampled across for hundreds of years by thousands of donkey's hooves and men's feet. It could have been worse though - he could have been face up! Across from the museum is a café which used to be the old bakery in Chora. Apart from being an interesting place to see, with its old ovens and baking equipment, you can view some of the outdoor exhibits in the museum opposite, but with a cool beer in hand. They have a rooftop dining area that is a charming setting, with a good view over the mountains and the refreshing sound of running water from a waterfall in the corner, surrounded by plants.

Chapter XV Farming and Donkeys

The Pagali Hotel, where our clients have now stayed since mid-2000, is a family owned hotel. It is set in the small and beautiful mountain village of Langada, away from the road and with a wonderful, warm and friendly atmosphere. From this vantage point, you can sit and watch the red sunset behind the mystical, uninhabited island of Nikouria, which lies above us to the west. People who have travelled the Greek islands extensively have told us that this is their favourite spot in the whole of Greece.

From the hotel you see the villagers going about their daily routine, riding their donkeys up and down the village steps, greeting and chatting with everyone as they pass. Throughout the summer months, the village is a mass of colour, with flowering bougainvillea, wisteria and jasmine. You can hear the donkeys braying in the fields and the singing cicadas in the olive groves beneath.

The restaurant is in a taverna style, where you can sit on the wide veranda, shaded from the sun by dense grape vines and wisteria, or inside in a warm room, surrounded by old family photographs and antiques. The food is renowned throughout the island. Nikos, the owner, insists on knowing the precise origin of all the ingredients, and most of the food is organic, much of it grown on the island. The choice of dishes is wide. You can enjoy fresh goat meat from the grill, village cheese from goat milk prepared in the traditional way on top of a wood fire, and local olive oil and wines. In the morning, you can smell the jasmine and the fresh bread coming out of the baker's oven next door, also owned by the family. Outside the taverna is a popular meeting place where the old men gather, drinking coffee and putting the world to rights or playing tavli, the ladies picking over olives or vine leaves in big bowls on the steps, making preparations for dinner. The location is very peaceful, but you should be ready for local musicians and lots of dancing on some evenings.

The Pagali hotel is known as an 'agri-tourist' Hotel. That is to say, it is primarily a farming company, and the hotel and taverna is related diversification. This works out very well, as much of the food is from their own farm. The pork, chicken, eggs, salads and vegetables are all organic and all grown on Amorgos. All the waste from the kitchen apart from the meat goes back to the animals, and so the cycle starts again. This is typical of Nikos' approach to the business. He is very much in command. In his early fifties, he still has a full head of hair and sometimes a beard, depending on how he feels. His slight paunch is the result of enjoying his own cuisine. Joanna, his delightful and attractive wife of just a few years now, looks considerably younger than him, with a hairstyle which changes every time she has a chance to justifiably spoil herself on the mainland. Neither are to be argued with and their fantastic staff are well aware of this. Nikos is your archetypal smooth-talking Greek guy. In the taverna, his female guests are all over him like a nasty rash, much to the chagrin of Joanna.

Nikos also has a fishing boat which helps to supplement the farm produce. His favourite quarry is shark. His record so far was a five metre, two hundred and seventy kilo, five-gilled shark. It was longer than his boat, and obviously too large to go inside, so it had to be towed halfway around the island to Aegiali. He didn't have a harpoon or shotgun with him with which to kill it. They managed to get the shark's chin onto the stern, but it wasn't very happy and was thrashing and gnashing dangerously, threatening to turn the boat over. The only way to control it was to get a rope around the tail and pull the tail onto the stern as well. There was only Nikos and his godfather, also a Nikos, on board. The operation took over an hour. When we saw it, we couldn't believe what they had achieved. The following day Nikos wanted to go out and find a bigger one, but no one would go with him.

At our end of the island there are very few fields. Most of the farming has to be done on terracing on the mountainsides. This is very labour intensive and extremely hard work, as it all has to be done by hand and with the help of donkeys. The terraces were built as long ago as the Fifth Century BC. The majority are now in disrepair, but some are still worked. Traditionally the farmers would grow a combination of wheat and barley in the same fields, using mixed seeds. There is evidence that this method of hedging against dry or wet weather has been going on since the Fifth Century BC. In dry weather, the barley does better than the wheat, and in wet springs, vice versa. Once the crop is cut using a scythe, it is tied into sheaves and piled so high onto donkeys that it looks as if there is no animal underneath. It appears that the harvest is moving down the narrow donkey paths of its own accord. Only when it gets closer can you see the nose of the donkey as he first turns his head to the left and then to the right, chewing for all his worth in a desperate attempt to lighten his load. As far as he is concerned, he is just carrying his own fuel, no different than a car or lorry consuming fuel as it proceeds.

In the next stage, the wheat is spread over a threshing circle, a stone-floored area surrounded by a low stone wall about ten metres in diameter. The grain then has to be separated from the chaff and straw. The well-fuelled donkeys are put to work on this duty, whereupon they begin to trample the crop to break it all up. Three or four donkeys are tied together in a very neat echelon starboard formation and led by a man who stands in the middle of the circle, just rotating on the spot. Of course, the inside donkey has an easy job of it, moving relatively slowly, but the poor old donkey on the outside knows that he has to move much faster. They all wear muzzles to prevent them from stopping for a further snack, but most of them have already eaten their fill whilst transporting the crop. Recently fed donkeys trampling grain present further problems as nature takes its course. Donkey droppings mashed into this combination firstly makes it difficult to separate the grain from the chaff and secondly affects the taste of the resultant produce, which is not popular with the islanders. This is where the Greek equivalent to lacrosse comes in. They cut the side off a gallon olive oil can and attach a stick to it to fashion a crude lacrosse stick. It is then the catcher's job to walk behind the donkeys and field any droppings, lobbing them over his shoulder into the field as he catches them. Again, it is not too much of a problem fielding from the inside donkey, but the catcher also knows the donkeys are each moving at a different speed and dreads a performance from the outside one. Of course the donkeys know well what goes on and consider it great fun to all perform at once. Being tied together in this close formation makes communication very easy. They model themselves on their heroes, 'The Red Arrows', and at the appropriate time the leader just bays 'dung on, dung on, go' and mayhem rains, along with all the droppings. This is when the game plan changes. The catcher now transfers his wide range of sporting skills from lacrosse to rugby. He dives across the straw to retrieve the small oblong rugby balls and tries to convert them before being trampled to death by the oncoming team, who by now are looking at him with little smirking faces.

With this operation successfully complete, the straw is raked from the circle, leaving the grain and chaff. A suitable wind is awaited and then the winnowing begins. The wind direction is indicated by a piece of grass tied to a stick at the side of the circle. There are higher tech models of this indicator, from thin pieces of plastic right up to a proper wind vane in use. We are just awaiting a cable drive and remote indicator to be installed, so the farmer doesn't even need to get out of bed to plan his programme for the day. With a suitable wind, the grain and chaff are thrown into the air, whereupon the lighter chaff blows out of the circle and the grain lands back in. The procedure is repeated until only grain remains.

Although no updated methods of winnowing have been spotted yet, there is a high tech version of threshing called a rotavator. These machines, imported from Athens, have been spotted clawing their way around the stone threshing circles. It is way beyond the maker's recommendations, as they were never designed to rotavate on stone slabs like large kitchen liquidisers, reducing the harvest to its component parts. The one and only local garage is very happy though, as they survey the line of machines on their forecourt awaiting repair for another punishing harvest next year. The donkeys are also ecstatic, although it does limit their opportunities for revenge on their owners.

At a press convention here in the spring of 2003, there were film crews and photographers as well as journalists. We offered to take them for a short walk up into the mountains. There was a considerable amount of equipment so we needed a donkey. I asked our friend Nikolas if we could borrow one of his more placid and obedient donkeys, that I would be able to manage on my own. He has many donkeys and mules. He uses them to transport building materials, olives, firewood, hay, gas bottles and other heavy shopping for people who live a distance from the road.

We were starting at nine o'clock the following day. Nikolas said he would be busy then, but would tie Limoni, the donkey, to the telephone booth in the car park in the village of Langada, where the press bus would stop and we would start our walk. Even though I have experience in loading and leading donkeys, I still felt honoured that he trusted me with something which, on this island, is a valuable asset and part of his livelihood. It is not like borrowing a friend's car. If I mismanaged the operation, the donkey could be injured. It would not be just a case of taking it to the nearest garage to be repaired. Injuries take time to heal, and at the worst the animal might have to be destroyed. As it was, Nikolas didn't need to worry. I left the hotel a few minutes ahead of the press bus in the Land Rover to prepare the donkey. I reached the car park to find the telephone booth unoccupied. There was not a man or donkey in sight. At the other end of the car park was a donkey tied to the rubbish skips. This one had no saddle or panniers fitted, so it was clearly not Limoni. By the telephone booth was another donkey in a field; this had a saddle but no panniers. I knew who owned the field and they confirmed that it was their steed. There are three car parks in the village of Langada. I ran to the next one down, no donkey. I ran to the bottom one, no unattended donkeys. I ran all the way back up to the top of the village, which is a considerable number of steps. I turned up in a bit of a state, completely dripping, as the press arrived in their air-conditioned coach with Henri in attendance. They took one look at me as if to say, 'So this is the roughie-toughie mountain guide'? 'He can't even walk from his Land Rover to the bus without getting into a lather'. With my leadership reputation already in ruins, it would have been good to demonstrate my organisational skills. I looked at all the camera equipment rolling off the bus. Movie cameras, TV cameras, huge still cameras with lenses so long that they almost reached to our destination. There were tripods, spare lenses, microphones and recorders. How was I going to explain that they would have to carry it all themselves, as the donkey had done a Houdini? What we

90

needed, failing the donkey, was a team of Sherpas. I looked around the square. Sherpas are just like Greek policemen, there's never one there when you need one. I tried to explain the situation to the assembled press. You would think that I'd just ruined their chances of getting a front page exclusive of Noel Coward in bed with Cleopatra. When I suggested that they should just carry their equipment themselves, they became most rude. They wouldn't be able to print words like that in their newspapers and journals. Half the equipment went back on the coach and we set off with the bare minimum. In the end, they all seemed to have a good morning out. Their problems were forgotten once we started to climb out of Langada and see the magnificent views of the mountains we were climbing, the peaks beyond and the shimmering blue water of the bay below.

Once we had seen our charges back onto the coach, we went to accost Nikolas. We sat at Nikos' taverna in the middle of the village, drinking well-earned cold beers and waiting for him to pass by. A far preferable strategy than rushing around this mountainous village looking for him. The first person who passed by was Yannis, Nikolas' father, who has since passed away. He said, 'Why did you not take Limoni'? I said, 'Because he wasn't there'. 'I put him there on the telephone kiosk at eight o'clock and he was still there at ten' he said, by now getting very agitated and upset. He was a delightful old gentleman and like most of the villagers, he liked to help people as much as he could. Our Greek is not brilliant so we couldn't suggest possible scenarios in detail. He just felt that he had let us down when he knew that he had done as requested. Fortunately, before Yannis could wind himself up into a fit inducing frenzy, Nikolas arrived. He speaks very good English. We explained the situation, with his father shouting in the background that he had done as he was asked. He told Nikolas that Limoni was there at eight and he saw him again at ten. I suggested that maybe the donkey had got loose and someone had tied it up again after nine o'clock. 'My father has been tying up donkeys for eighty years' said Nikolas. 'His knots do not become loose'. It briefly crossed my mind that the donkey was only tied up after nine. Most local people have no idea of time, just sunrise and sunset. Unless they are catching a ship, they do not usually even know what day it is – every day is the same here. Nikolas was in charge of this and he is very reliable and punctual, so this was not the answer. 'What if someone borrowed it before nine and put it back afterwards'? I said. Neither Nikolas nor his father would accept this. There was a general pause for thought. This was broken by Yannis, who had decided that they had better get to the bottom of this quandary. There were three of their donkeys with him. 'Which one of these three was it that was missing this morning'? Yannis said. He had the satisfied look of Hercule Poirot when he knows he has just solved the crime. I looked puzzled. He pointed at one and said 'Do you recognise this donkey'? I couldn't tell if the look on Nikolas' face was amazement or admiration for his father's initiative in solving the mystery. 'How can I recognise a donkey that wasn't there'? I reasoned. He still wouldn't stand the ID parade down though and continued to pursue his line of investigation. Eventually he threw his hands in the air and walked off, dismissing us as stupid foreigners who couldn't recognise a donkey. We agreed with Nikolas that the whole episode was indeed a conundrum. Two days later, Nikolas came up to us. 'The donkey was borrowed' he said. 'I have spoken to the person involved, it will never happen again'. Nikolas and his family are powerful on this island. It will never happen again!

Titi had been living on the island, mainly in the summers, for fifteen years. She had to walk with a stick due to a very bad car accident many years ago, and therefore had difficulty getting to some of the more remote areas that we take our clients to. She loved the island, as everyone does, and wanted to see as much of it as possible, but had never been to Agii Saranda (Forty Saints). This is a particularly beautiful bay with turquoise-blue sea and a very special church. This structure is a small, double church where the left-hand chapel has been maintained over the years, but the right-hand side is the gem.

I needed to take the Land Rover to the other side of the island to drop off Henri and some clients at a point where there is a track from which a four wheel drive vehicle can just make it to a point above the bay. They were on a long walk around the area. After we had dropped them off, Titi and I went to visit some old friends of hers who had a taverna at the other end of the island. The elderly gentleman had been a fisherman and had scrimped and saved for many years to earn the money to build this taverna. To remind him of the source of his wealth, he kept his old fishing boat alongside the premises. It was not much bigger than a rowing boat found on a boating lake, but considerably less sea worthy. The gaps between the wooden planking of the hull were now so large that they were almost as wide as the planking itself. If placed on the water, it would certainly need a stop watch calibrated in 100ths of a second to measure its time above water before it became the first Greek fishing submarine. There was, however, no doubt that it was once a magnificent little traditional fishing boat, and he showed it to us with pride and tears in his eyes. Titi asked if she could buy it from him. He said that he would sell her his heart, but never his boat. After a few ouzos, which were pretty unavoidable with Titi in tow, we drove to the top of the bay of Agii Saranda. We walked the last mile or so down to the shore. We actually didn't have a good set of legs between us, as I had strained a tendon in my right foot whilst out running two days previous, and Titi's right leg was not good. Indeed, her right knee was completely fused, so she walked and drove, which was even more exciting, with a stiff leg. Together we limped very slowly to the bottom, actually passing Henri with our clients on their way up. Titi took many photographs of the flowering bushes and the springs on the way. We then had the tricky bit of working our way on our sticks up to the church of Agii Saranda. We made it without either of us falling over. Our arrival apparently required celebration, because from her small rucksack out came a bottle of ouzo! After all, it was by now midday and perfectly acceptable to have a snifter. When we were suitably refreshed, I showed her the first church with its beautiful icons depicting the forty saints and various crosses and ornaments all immaculately maintained. She spent some time in there buying and lighting multitudes of candles and incense burners and by the time she had finished, the wonderful little church looked as if it had been prepared for a Christmas carol service. We came out into the sunlight and when I led her into the second chapel, I was pleased that she was absolutely taken aback by what we saw.

It is covered in dust and cobwebs and there are no icons or candles, just the basic chapel as it was abandoned hundreds of years ago. Fourth Century BC Corinthian columns abound. The altar, supported by these, is a marble slab from the same period. The church has been renovated over the years and features historic pieces dating back thousands of years. There are these original, recycled building materials, probably from Akro Kastri, Venetian arches and even a small amount of relatively new concrete. It is an absolute wealth of history through the ages.

We went back outside and this discovery required further celebration. After another ouzo, I went a little way up the mountainside to take some photographs. When I returned, Titi had gone. I found her back in the old chapel taking in the amazing features, perched on the altar with a cigarette in one hand, ouzo in the other and her stiff leg stuck out in front of her! After a little more time, we made our way back to the Land Rover and negotiated the various slopes, crevices and bends, utilizing the vehicle to the limits. This was not easy, but made more difficult as I was forced to operate one-handed, as ouzos were passed across the cab to me. A great day was had by all. Well, Titi and I had a good day. Henri and our clients looked very hot and tired when we met up with them; we couldn't think why.

As mentioned before, cars were a fairly new commodity on the island, and some of the islanders were still not one hundred percent sure what to push and shove to get them to do what they want. Personally I find them easier to control than donkeys. When drivers here are under pressure, they do tend to get slightly unpredictable. A local was rushing to catch the ferry one week, but unfortunately missed it, literally, and ended up in the drink. Luckily, no one was seriously hurt, but the extracted, salt water marinated car was sure going to be a challenge to the local garage. A book was opened on the months involved, and personally we said, never. I think that we were correct. The driver could be excused for becoming confused about the orientation of the harbour, as the quay in Ormos Aegialis is a relatively new acquisition. The ferries used to come in and anchor in the bay and small fishing boats would go out and ferry the people and goods ashore. This included donkeys, goats and cattle which were winched between the ship and the fishing boat.

A friend of ours recounts the time when she was being pulled on board the ship from a fishing boat. 'It was winter and I was in a thick woollen suit, with a suitcase in my hand. I somehow lost my grip with my free hand and ended up in the freezing water with a huge splash. I was dragged out, still with my suitcase, and hauled on board. I sploshed my way into the purser's office, dripping water all over his carpet. He didn't say a word. He just handed me a glass of Metaxa (Greek brandy) as the pool of water around me grew larger'.

At that time the water came right up to the tavernas and a little chapel at the front of the village, and the fishing boats would just be pulled up onto the beach. In those days it was a busier harbour than it is now, as the easiest way to get from one end of the island to the other was by boat. Indeed, the two harbours were treated almost as two different islands, with all the ferries from Piraeus calling in at both. The road between the two ports was only completed in 1998. Before then, to go by land involved a five hour donkey ride through the mountains. We still follow that route with some of our fitter clients. All the children from Aegiali who went to the high school in Chora, the capital, used to have to do this every Monday and Saturday and stay at the school during the week. The harbour was built in 1985 to enable the municipality to bring in the equipment, such as poles and cable, to install electricity to our end of the island. Chora and Katapola had enjoyed this luxury since 1956. From 1989, all of the main villages have had electricity. It is generated on the island by a diesel run plant in Katapola and is 'quite' reliable.

One of the walks on our programme is between two Fifth Century BC cities, Akro Kastri and Minoa. The walk follows the most ancient road on the island between these two cities and past Agii Saranda, mentioned earlier. It is a particularly beautiful walk in the summer, as it goes through spring fed valleys with flowering trees and bushes, and even in the spring, trickling water can still be heard. Both cities are in spectacular locations in prominent positions overlooking the sea, enabling sight of any imminent invasion. The land around Akro Kastri is still worked in the age-old manner, as is has been since the city was built. In the old city, blocks of stone from the original buildings can still be seen, and old wells and farm buildings from more recent centuries surround the area. On the way to Minoa, we pass through an area in which evidence of Neolithic man has been found and is almost certainly the site of the first settlement on the island. Minoa is the more interesting of the two cities, as it has been subject to a number of archaeological digs from the middle of the 1800s to the present time. Temples and statues have been uncovered. Stairways and buildings can be seen and the Fifth Century BC lavatory to the gymnasium (high school) has been reconstructed. It is a communal affair with room for six sitting in a circle facing each other, with a wonderful view across the valley, and was probably a favourite meeting place in its day. We have been going to this site for many years; and sitting on the ancient loo never ceases to amuse me.

Chapter XVI Tourists

High season officially begins in mid-July, but the tourists start to arrive in force at the beginning of the month and it starts to get quiet again at the end of August. It is nothing like Corfu or Rhodes, but we don't particularly like it. We prefer a quiet and peaceful island. However tourism is the main source of income for the island these days. Many of the visitors here during high season are Greek. There are considerable price increases in a number of areas and indeed some of the small hotels only open for these six weeks. Many are owned by fishermen who now turn their skills from extracting money from fish to extracting money from tourists, both of which have their slippery qualities. Small blocks of rooms that looked abandoned and scruffy are suddenly brought to life. The shutters are thrown open, gallons of whitewash appear and people climb all over the structures, turning them into gleaming white buildings with blue shutters. Signs go up saying Petros' Pension, Stavros' Rooms and other equally imaginative names. At this time of year if you are a painter and decorator, you are in more demand than a blood donor at a bullfight. There are a few people on the island who make a living as painters, including a British gentleman called Len who has been here for many years. When he first said that he was a painter, we assumed of the artistic kind until we noticed that he always came down from the mountains at the end of a day's work covered in white paint. The conclusion being that either he specializes in arctic scenes or does a lot of whitewashing; given our location we correctly assumed the latter. This line of work is considerably more lucrative on this island than the artistic kind. The islanders are still very traditional and all the houses have blue shutters and doors and white stonework. The little villages in blue and white gleaming in the sun contrast beautifully with the ruggedness of the mountains beyond. The traditional blue and white comes from the times of Turkish occupation, when flying the Greek flag was forbidden. In defiance of the occupying force, the Greeks painted their houses in the same colour as their flag. The whitewash comes in large tins or bags from Athens these days, but traditionally they used to make their own. In the mountains there are some very prickly bushes which look like crumpled up chicken wire. It is Greek spiny spurge or Euphorbia acanthothamnos. It is not advisable to fall into one of these because you end up simulating a pincushion. I can vouch for this first hand. These bushes were taken and put into specially built stone circles, some of which can still be seen up in the mountains. They were then burnt down to a fine white ash that was mixed with water to form the whitewash.

Some of the fishermen who do not own hotels don't bother fishing during the high season, either. They take people from the two main harbours or other small fishing settlements out to secluded beaches and islands that the little darlings would otherwise have to swim or walk to. As a result, the quiet secluded beaches are no longer quiet and secluded, so why go there? A few of the trendier bars put their prices up during this period; fortunately they are very few in number. They claim that the suppliers increase prices at this time of year, but this is incorrect. A classic little trick they have is to increase the price of a bottle of beer from three to four euros ('just a small percentage increase!' they say.) On closer inspection, the bottle size has also changed from half a litre to a third of a litre - a considerable percentage increase in cost. The traditional cafeneions where the elderly gentlemen of the village pass their time and the few small bars that stay open all year still charge the same very low prices and have a far better atmosphere than their money grabbing, part-time contemporaries.

The old chief of police walked into a café. Presuming it was an ordinary visit, the owner primed a large carafe of wine for him. However it was an official visit, to inspect the owner's licence to operate. Now this was a bit tricky, as they didn't actually have one. An old one from the previous owner used to hang on the wall over the cash machine, but this had been removed awaiting new papers from Naxos. In its place was a new calendar with a very nice photograph of the establishment. The chief had seen the licence there many times before, even if he hadn't inspected it closely. They passed the inspection with flying colours, despite the lack of licence. Instead of leaving with boring old official papers, the chief departed clutching a nice new calendar for his office, leaving a blank space on the café wall.

One summer, our organizational abilities were stretched to the limit and we almost used up as much international airtime on the mobile as the time an idiot sent me a 1.8 megabyte e-mail. Our clients this summer, before we used the Pagali hotel, were a British couple, both academics. We got up at 04.00 to see them onto the hotel bus to take them to the other port of Katapola. After I'd eventually extracted the driver from his coffee and some deep meaningful conversation with a blonde bimbo, who had probably just fallen out of a nightclub, we got them on their way. At 06.00 we had a call from our clients to say that the Skopelitis, their ferry, had not sailed, and no one really seemed to know when it was going to do so. The earliest time offered was 09.00, which would result in a missed connection in Naxos and a missed flight. The driver had apparently just dumped them without checking this information and presumably made a dash back for the blonde. I rang the hotel's 'twenty-four hour' reception to get the driver back, but there was no answer. We leapt into the Land Rover and picked them up ourselves, returning them an hour later to the hotel.

I had no time to find and kill the driver - that could wait until I had time to enjoy it. There were various options to recover the situation, some dodgy, relying on almost certainly delayed ferries and flights, and others rock solid. From experience we went for the rock solid. Four hours later, we had them booked onto a later ferry all the way to Athens, into a hotel overnight at the airport and on a new flight the following morning back to Heathrow. They understood Greek ferries and appreciated all that we had done for them. I took them down to the ferry, this time in our port of Aegiali, not trusting the hotel driver to do it properly. The ferry was exactly on time, absolutely amazing. There were a number of cars and motor bikes waiting to be boarded, a process which takes some time, so I was more than happy to go on board with them and show them where they could store their bags safely on the car deck and say our good-byes. By now all the passengers were loaded, but cars were still on the quay. I glanced over my shoulder to notice the ramp lifting and the ship pulling away. I didn't hang around to ask why, it was a bit obvious to me, and there was no way I was going to spend a total of twenty hours on a ferry and a night in Athens. I made a dash for it weaving my way through the various members of the ship's crew trying to get in my way and jumped. Upon landing, quite safely, on the quay, I noticed the ship's captain down there giving instructions on the repositioning of the ferry to make it easier to load the cars. Well, how was I to know, and it was his fault for screwing up in the first place.

At the back of the line of cars waiting to go on was a little hire car, belonging to the hotel, being steered by Nikitas, the hotel owner, and pushed by one of his drivers. That's delegation for you! They didn't have nine months to spare and were sending it to Naxos for repair. The ramp is quite steep so I lent a hand. When all the able-bodied cars were loaded, we were told to push aboard the cripple. They then gave us instructions for parking to keep it out of the way, until arrival in Naxos, where it would be off-loaded by the garage. We pushed and shoved it into place. I knew the ferry wasn't going to sail with us on board, because even though nothing had been said, I knew there was no way Nikitas would be leaving his island. It had been years since the last time he left, and he had sworn he would never do it again. He doesn't like the outside world but he loves his island. I was aware, yet again, of the by now familiar feeling of the ramp rising and the ferry starting to pull away. Amid much shouting and waving of arms, this time three of us had to run and jump for it, and this time the ferry really did depart for Athens. It had been a close one, which required a calming beer.

I went to see Vangelis at Celini, and it turned out that our clients who I'd just seen off had been teaching him yet more English slang. This time it was 'on the slate'. My heart fell. I knew they liked going there for nightcaps, but they were great people and surely hadn't left us to pay their slate. I pressed Vangelis for further details, bracing myself for the amount, while I watched the ship disappearing over the horizon. Vangelis smiled as he pulled a large denomination note off the wall with the words 'on the slate' written across it. They had very kindly credited our account to the tune of numerous beers. We could do with more clients like this! Suitably refreshed after a few free beers, I went to the hotel to kill the driver, but I was too late. He'd been sacked.

We got an e-mail from our clients informing us that all the rearranged plans we had made to get them home had worked. It was nice of them to give us this feedback. They had been a great couple to walk with and for two academics were surprisingly normal and quite fascinating to talk to. Although he had a PhD in computer science and she was a historian they had an unnatural fascination with donkeys and their saddles. It turned out that they had two donkeys at home and were very interested in getting the two overfed and pampered animals to do some work around their farm. To do this, they needed to know the design of a donkey saddle. There was no point in having them made here, as the donkeys on the island are apparently considerably slimmer than their podgy layabouts in England. The whole week turned into an information gathering and data collection exercise. He actually arrived on the island as 'Doctor' and left as 'Professor', though I believe it was due to a telephone call from his university and nothing to do with donkey saddle research. No doubt by the time they had spent ten hours on a ferry, all the data was collated, classified and cross referenced and a thesis half-written. We had to examine every donkey and saddle we saw or passed, and on Amorgos, the donkey population is considerable. The size and weight of the wood and padding had to be assessed. The type and means of attaching said saddle had to be logged. The length and type of connections on the harness had to be noted. The digital camera was brought out and every angle of every piece was photographed. Also the donkeys, modelling all the latest fashion accessories, had to be photographed from every possible vantage point. The hotel owner's father made the mistake of parking his donkey in the car park and this became the subject of much in-depth research. Fortunately he didn't come out as the animal's behind was being photographed because I'm sure he would never have believed the explanation even if we had pointed out that they were academics on holiday.

But it didn't stop there. They wanted to saddle their donkeys to work, not to ride. The saddle can be used to sit on, but is also used to attach a number of accessories. There were two types of accessory they were particularly interested in.

These may be the subject of a further thesis or just appendices of the first. The first accessories are for carrying bulky loads such as boxes. They consist of two platforms fitted one on either side of the saddle. They are like small wooden stretchers and sit almost horizontally, but angled slightly inwards so the load does not slip off. They are suspended from each end of the top piece of the saddle and a crossing-over strap stops them from swinging. The second accessory is for carrying loose loads such as grain, sand or pebbles. This is rather ingenious. Two beer crates are taken and their insides and bottoms are removed to leave just the outside shell. The bottom is cut out of a sack, placed inside the crate and tied around the top so that you have a hessian tube dangling out of the bottom of the crate. The bottom of the tube is then tied up to form a bag with the top kept rigid by the crate. Each crate is then tied, one to either side of the donkey. The bag is then filled with the load and transported to its destination. Upon arrival, the bottom of the bag is untied and all the contents drop out, much to the relief of the donkey.

There are two carpenters in Langada who specialize in making saddles, and it is a little confusing because they are both called Michalis. Usually, like in Wales, where you have Jones the fish, and Lewis the spanner, here it is Nikos the sailor, Stephanas the butcher, and so on. Michalis the saddle does not help. Fortunately one is much older than the other, and the younger one is very rarely sober, so they can be differentiated by age and posture. We thought we gathered just about all there was to know about donkey saddles and their accessories when an antique saddle by the side of the fireplace at the hotel was spotted. This was an adjustable one which would allow for the expansion and contraction of a donkey, presumably allowing for both famine and feast. Out came the measuring stick, the digital camera, the notebook, the Geiger counter and the electron microscope. They nearly missed the ferry over that one.

Traditionally in Greece, you name your children after their grandparents. Your first son is named after the paternal grandfather and your second after the maternal grandfather. The first daughter is named after the maternal grandmother and the second daughter after the paternal grandmother, and after that it is a free for all. However, the discretionary names are usually saint's names, not 'Tinkerbell' or 'Tyrone'. Although this custom is not strictly adhered to these days throughout Greece it is closely followed on Amorgos, which takes pride in its traditions.

This means that if Maria has four daughters and each of them have a daughter, there will be five Marias in the family. Given that a name like Maria is a popular name in Greece, if they have a family lunch and invite a few friends with their families, there could be twenty Marias at the table. 'Please pass the salt, Maria', could result in a rugby scrum. For this reason, many children are given nicknames or a variation to their given name is used. Maria, for example, could be called Mary or Maraki. Stephanos could adopt the name Stephanas or Stephanakis. Dimitris is often called Mimis. The female equivalent to this name is Dimitria. Variations to this are Dimitroula, Maroula, Roula or even Marouli which is actually the Greek for lettuce! And, so it goes on. It is worth noting that most male names end in an 'S'. If you are referring to said gentleman, you would sound the 'S', but when talking to him you would not. The latter in grammatical terms is known as the vocative tense. For example, my name in Greek is 'Pavlos'. You would say, 'That book Pavlos wrote is a load of bullshit'. However you would say to me, 'Pavlo, that book of yours is an absolute gem'. Got the idea? Please note that I do have a black belt in the ancient art of origami.

Chapter XVII Journalists, Computers and Naxos

Peter Hughes, a renowned and prize winning travel writer, arrived here on holiday with his partner Bronwyn. Henri found them standing by our Land Rover and they started asking her about our operation here. I arrived wanting to know what these 'nosy parkers' were after. When he explained who he was, I said 'My dear chap!' We offered to take them to see a few places that visitors don't normally see and we were delighted when they accepted. We took them to Theologos and on towards Stavros. Peter kept stressing that he was here on holiday and not to work, but he couldn't resist it. It was only a very short time before the notebook came out, and by the end of the morning they were so thrilled with the 'hidden Amorgos' that we were subjected to the third degree about our programme. My resistance to interrogation techniques from my Royal Air Force days worked well for the first few minutes. Name, rank and number followed by; 'I cannot answer that question, Sir'. Then they played dirty and bought us beer. They never covered that in training, so we gave in and told them everything, well almost. Many years later we made contact with Peter again to ask if he would be kind enough to write a foreword to our Visitor's and Walker's Guide to Amorgos. We were delighted when he agreed and very humbled by his kind words. We were also saddened to hear that Bronwyn had passed away shortly after that holiday. However she had loved the Greek islands, had never been to Amorgos before, but in Peter's words, 'she was on an eternal quest to find her favourite. Amorgos was the last Greek island she visited and one of the most memorable'.

Our computer decided that enough was enough. It had been carted across Europe, bounced over the rough terrain of the island, thrown about in force eight gales on Greek ferries and operated in the office just a few yards from the shore in an atmosphere which could salt peanuts by just throwing them into the air. It totally refused access to the Office Suite and told us that the sending of e-mails was an illegal activity and was going to shut down, presumably, out of respect for the law. There are four critical drivers in our operation. Firstly our legs, secondly the Land Rover, thirdly the mobile phone and, last but not least, the computer. I had just pulled a ligament running. The mobile objected to being left outside all night in the salty atmosphere and didn't work for a while. The Land Rover developed a nasty rattle and a blowing manifold at the same time. Both were due to the cowboy suppliers missing out a small component called a nut, which could be easily fixed but was a worry at the time. So it was not unreasonable that the computer should consider that it was about time to become the centre of attention. We reloaded Windows three times, but to no avail. We tried every other trick in the book, but it wasn't going to play ball. It learnt some new Greek words not found in the dictionary and got a very severe reprimand, but still would not get off its backside. We even ordered it some new Microsoft 2000 software, promising to load it as soon as it arrived (I didn't say that it could take months). We left it closed down overnight to contemplate its possible demise and options available, but still no go.

With only a few computers on the island at the time, there was not much call for an IT specialist. The blacksmith is a dab hand at shoeing horses, trimming donkey's hooves, cutting people's hair and helping out with the olive press next door, but computers are not his strong point. In fact, he is under the impression that a 'computer' is someone who travels to work like the farmer from up in the mountains at Asphondilitis who lives in Potamos and rides his donkey on the three hour round-trip journey to work each day. There were no Internet cafes on Amorgos or any other means of access available to us at that time. We were cut off from the outside electronic mail world and had no means of running the operation except by pen and paper. There was nothing for it, we had to go to Naxos and return on the next ferry that was fortunately leaving the next day and not a week later. We knew the Skopelitis left at 07.00 and on one occasion had taken us nine hours, so we deliberately made our decision after it had passed the bottom of our garden when it was too late.

We decided to take the 11.00 Hermes, which normally only takes five hours or so depending which islands it calls in at. Reporting to the ferry office when it opened at 10.00, we were informed that the Hermes had left at 06.00 that morning, but there was a 'Supercat' at 12.30 from Katapola that only takes about an hour. We thought we would believe it when we saw it, but booked anyway. The problem with these high-tech, high-speed vessels is that they are very weather limited, but that day the weather was excellent, so we thought that we would risk it. We had seen these high-speeds from a distance before, but never close up. When the Supercat eventually arrived, it was a very impressive, sleek looking vessel, and inside was extremely comfortable, with seating fourteen across in airline type seats and a steward drinks and food service if required. There was an on-board movie and all mod cons. We pulled out of Katapola and on went the power, to say it moved would be an understatement. Being used to the old Greek ferries, it was like being on Concord compared to a Dakota. I went in search of the maker's nameplate, '1998 Cowes, Isle of White UK'. I sat back with satisfaction and pride to watch some American trash on the movie screen, wondering why the ship builders hadn't built in some decent British movies. With nothing else to do as the islands whistled past, I was getting quite involved with the movie as the man-built robots were building bigger and better robots and about to take over the world when 'her indoors' ordered me off the boat. We were in Naxos in just forty five minutes, absolutely amazing. I wasn't allowed to stay on to Athens to see the end of the film, so now I will never know if mankind is to survive the robot invasion or not. Only time will tell.

The computer shop was to close at 16.30 for two hours, so we made a beeline for it and we were pleased to find a very respectable looking establishment in the commercial area of Naxos. Archetypal young computer boffins in jeans, tee shirts and trainers manned it. There was quite clearly one chap in charge who all the lackeys turned to before pressing a single button or blowing their noses. One said lackey, who was worked by remote control from the big cheese, assured me that it was a very small problem that could be resolved quickly. After fifteen minutes, the replacement of two system files and the handing over of about fifteen pounds, which we felt was a little steep for a Greek island, we left for our hotel. We had instructions to load Windows one more time and this would solve all our problems. We did as instructed, only to find we were back in the same old pickle. It was now 16.30, siesta time.

At 18.30, we were sitting on their doorstep with laptop in hand. The next six hours were a real test of our patience. Not only did they sell and repair computers and software, but they also ran a computerised sign-writing business. One by one the lackeys had a go at fixing our problem, one by one they fell by the wayside and in our opinion compounded the problem. In the end the boss had to take over. With lackeys surrounding the Guru to see how he was going to get out of this one, and me trying to get a glimpse of what was going on as more and more of my valued files disappeared down the tubes, time marched on. The Guru was talking on a cordless phone constantly, shouting orders to his men and rushing in and out to oversee the logo-ing of a pizza van outside. Henri went outside on one occasion to blow a gasket to see him appear just in time to stop the graphics of a pizza oven being stuck on upside down. At about 21.00, his very harassed young wife arrived to tell him that his kleftiko had been fed to the goats and if he didn't come home soon, he could find himself another wife. For the next hour, he massaged the computer with one hand and his wife's body with the other, as his men shoved various phones under his chin so he could talk to all and sundry. His wife eventually left, but he then spent another hour pacifying her on the phone, all the time hammering away with the spare hand, swapping, deleting, altering and rewriting files. Every time he thought he'd fixed it, another error message would come up again. There was no swearing or cursing, each time he would gently tap the desk, smile and try something else. He was like a salmon fisherman after the king of the river, he was actually enjoying himself. At midnight, just as I was wondering about the scrap value of a melted down laptop, he announced that he had beaten it and invited me to admire his work and take it for a test drive. I took it round a few sharp bends as hard as I could and pushed it to the limits. All was working well, but the entire contents of our address book had disappeared. We were so relieved and knackered that I told him not to worry about it; it would be a morning's work to reinstall, but what the heck. He wouldn't have any of it and insisted on trying to recover the data. At 00.30 we insisted that it really wasn't a problem and we wanted to eat what would be our first proper meal in over twenty four hours. We asked him how much we owed, reminding him that we had already paid some money that morning. Considering that this was for fifteen minutes work and he had just spent a further six hours working on it, we braced. He said the equivalent of six pounds more. Henri got the money out of the coffers so fast before he changed his mind that she got confused with the denominations and gave him less than he had asked for. He said not to worry, that would be fine. We shook hands and left, physically and emotionally drained. As we looked back, he was sitting at another screen tapping away and talking on the phone, presumably to his long suffering wife.

After breakfast the following day, I started reloading software and reconfiguring the infrared mobile phone link before the computer shop reopened, if indeed it had ever closed. It all worked a dream. Our next mission was to return to Amorgos. On arrival in Naxos, we had been to see our friends at Naxos Travel who we use as our ticketing agents on the island. The obvious ferry to return on was the Georgios Express which left at 11.30 and took about five hours. When we explained why we were in Naxos with no clients this time, they felt sorry for us and gave us a fifty percent discount on the fare. It was peak tourist season and Naxos is much busier than Amorgos. We knew it was going to be pretty chaotic on the quay, but nothing could have prepared us for what awaited us. It was as if the Dunkirk evacuation and D-day landings were both taking place on the same date at the same small place. Hundreds of people and vehicles were trying to get off the island and the same numbers were trying to invade. Only this time, every nationality was involved on both sides and it was every man, woman and child for themselves. There were backpackers with an interesting variety of wares hanging from their persons. The image of imminent invasion was compounded by some wearing not only backpacks but small front packs as well, which looked like Second World War reserve parachutes. Some had beach balls strapped on, others had rackets, there was even a youngster carrying a small pair of oars, goodness knows where the boat was stashed. This would have worried the fishermen of Amorgos, as their token effort towards securing their small tenders from budding young pirates, in the tourist season, is to remove the oars. There were Greeks dressed as if they had just stepped out to do some shopping in Knightsbridge, alongside objects that had quite clearly been beamed in from the sixties. Some of these youngsters had long, unwashed, unkempt hair, earrings and beads, wearing colourful wrap-around skirts and blouses - and these were just the chaps! Others looked as if they were old enough to know better and were probably leftovers from the sixties. If they had any idea what year it was, which is doubtful, they appeared as if they didn't care anyway. There was a man carrying two cages containing his budgerigars and people with numerous dogs on leads. Hotel owners mixed with the crowds carrying pictures of their establishments to entice people into staying there, and travel reps stalked around trying to get a whiff of their quarry. A British travel film crew was on location, covering a chubby young couple with even chubbier rucksacks touring the islands. A family of four arrived on one small motor bike, there was an elderly gentleman being pushed around in a wheelchair looking rather bemused and two nuns who seemed to be going around making sure everyone was OK. The only people missing were the WRVS.

Lorries, cars, vans, taxis, motorbikes, pickup trucks, coaches and buses weren't segregated from the passengers, they just picked their way amongst the crowds on the quay. Some vehicles had trailers, others large roof racks and some both. One even had a trailer on a roof rack, presumably trying to save on ferry charges. There were windsurfers, cases, bicycles, boats and even a chest of draws on roofs. Boats, fridges, boxes and piles of bricks in trailers. Trying to control this mayhem were a handful of port police, accompanied by their very impressive looking chief who had the gold scrambled egg on his hat and more gold bars on his shoulder than a Russian general. The means of control is to blow a whistle until you are purple in the face and wave your arms around simulating a gyrocopter trying to get airborne in a force eight gale. Combined with the sound of vehicle engines, motorbikes were revving up as if they were just about to do an Evel Knievel across the gap between the quay and the ship's ramp as it reversed in. People were shouting to try and get their groups together and by some miracle all catch the same boat, but it was not the whistles that could be heard over all of this, but the ubiquitous mobile phone. Every Greek has one, and in such a large enclosed group, whenever a ringing tone is heard, everyone starts punching buttons on their phone and shouting into the mouthpiece. It has not been unknown for people to have found themselves having a very confusing high decibel conversation with a person beside them thinking that they are digitally connected only to find the call was for a person one metre away now speaking quite coherently with Hong Kong. It is all very good for networking though and Greeks will make the most of any business opportunity.

The reason for the frenzied activity on the quay is due to Naxos being a hub for this part of the Aegean. The result of this is not only a heaving port on shore but also an ocean full of a wide ranging number of passenger and vehicle vessels. There are catamarans, hydrofoils, small and large ferries. These break down into High-Speed Cats, Seacats, Supercats and Flying Dolphins. Express ferries, local ferries and just plain old slow ferries, which are all now called 'express' just to fool the enemy. In the thirty minutes we were on the quay, the arrivals and departures included two Dolphins, one Seacat, one Supercat, one High-Speed Cat, three Express ferries and one local ferry. At one point there was a Supercat, an Express Ferry, a High-Speed Cat and a Flying Dolphin (a fast, aged hydrofoil), all loading and unloading at the same time from the same small quay. In the midst of all this ocean of activity, small yachts were bravely trying to depart the harbour, each time encountering the wrath of the next incoming vessel a hundred times their size. This results in the larger vessel giving one long blast on its horn that even drowns out the mobile phones. This internationally recognised signal officially means, 'Please get out of my way as I have restricted room to manoeuvre,' but one feels that the sentiment behind it is rather less polite. The High-Speed Cat is a big bastard. To expedite the offload of passengers, they put them all on the lower car deck so that when the ramp is lowered they can all troop off 20 abreast. As they stream off blinking in the bright sunlight, the scene is reminiscent of a science fiction film as the aliens return our people to earth. When your vessel is imminent, a chalkboard indicates which line to stand in. Blue wooden railings separate the three lines. By this time, everyone is happy to sit down and lean against them. The railings had only been painted a few months previous when we were there on another visit. On that occasion, we were amazed at the number of people who, on board, were all wearing similar tee-shirts, all sporting blue vertical stripes! We eventually boarded our ferry, the Georgios Express, again a British vessel, but this one was built in 1965. It is just forty kilometres from Naxos to Amorgos and we were very glad to be on this 'express' service as it only took five hours! We settled down in the ominously named 'distinguished class' lounge, leaving the tourists to find themselves suitable deck space to sun bathe. We reflected on the chaos on the quay and the potential for very serious accidents and frayed tempers, particularly given the high temperatures. There were neither. Everyone chatted amicably and helped each other out with luggage or directions. There was no hooting of horns or shouting, except into mobile phones. Everyone was taking their turn to proceed towards their nominated vessel. Even the French were being patient.

As part of the 'fix,' the computer engineer loaded Norton Utilities, a program that not only troubleshoots but also fine-tunes the system. I thought that I would take advantage of this 'free' software and fine tune the computer system. The whole computer froze up and I had to reload Windows yet again and reconfigure the mobile phone software. It all took six hours. I guess I will not do that again.

After arriving at the port of Aegiali, we went up to Tholaria to have a beer with the locals and get away from the tourists. Elias, who owns the olive press there and who we see quite often in the mountains tending his fields, was having a problem. He came round the corner from his house with a slack rope in his hand which suddenly went taut, he turned and started to pull as hard as he could on a hidden, immovable object, shouting and cursing. Suddenly the rope slackened, much to his surprise. His donkey trotted around the corner quite nonchalantly, as if to say, 'I just needed a little more time to get ready to face the world.' Elias picked himself up off the ground. His olive press was one of the very few remaining old presses in use on the island and a real piece of industrial archaeology. It was located in a small barn which was blackened with the soot from the open fires used to boil the water for the process. Each family took their olives to him in clearly marked sacks, and when he had acquired enough to offer some economies of scale, he started the process. Taking each family's batch in turn, he tipped them onto a large raised stone circle about two metres across and spread them out. A large stone roller pivoted in the centre of the circle was then rotated around to crush the olives. This was driven around by a donkey harnessed to the wooden arm through the centre of the roller. The pulp was then scooped out and placed into a large trough. Boiling water was poured in and it was all mixed together into a paste. Donkey-hair blankets were then laid on the side and the paste shovelled onto these, which were then folded over to form a square parcel. This package was then placed under a large cast iron press. This was then wound down by hand to press out all the liquid from the paste. This liquid, a mixture of oil and water, ran along a channel under the stone floor into a shallow pit. The oil and water were left to separate and the oil scooped off the top into tins, the water remaining in a sump at the bottom of the pit. The oil was then given to the families, minus a percentage that the press owner kept as payment for the service. The cakes of pressed olives were removed from the blankets and dried. These were then fed to the donkeys. Presumably the one doing all the work got the first choice, although he did prefer it when they used the press to process grapes! It is not so traditional these days. EU regulations say that oily water can't be allowed to run down the street. All the olives now go to a boring mechanical press. It is more efficient, but not as colourful.

Chapter XVIII Gypsies

From June through to September, the gypsies are regular visitors to Amorgos. They travel between the islands selling their wares from very large and overloaded trucks. Their target segment is the hotels and restaurants, and their marketing strategy has been cleverly developed through experience over the years. In June, when tavernas are just setting up for the season, their lorry is piled high with precarious towers of stacked plastic chairs and tables which perfectly demonstrate the physics of centrifugal forces as they negotiate the many hairpin bends on the island. The tall plastic towers turn into a banana shape, first to the left and then to the right, occasionally reducing in size as the centrifugal forces overcome the forces of friction and yet another plastic chair is catapulted down the mountain side into a herd of goats. The goats are fairly bemused about these plastic meteorites raining down from space, and although they have not yet perfected the art of sitting on them and ordering ouzo, they do find them useful shade from the midday sun.

As the season progresses, the essential fixed assets of setting up a taverna switch to less tangible wares, such as mops, buckets, tablecloths and towels. As business starts to get underway, their lorry tours the island loaded with boxes of mineral water, tons of garlic and other vegetables. Every self-respecting restaurateur has a collection of old olive oil cans and other used containers full of flowering geraniums to make the outside dining area more attractive. However, the competition between the few establishments is fierce and anything to improve the 'pulling power' and make the place look more attractive at this time of year is worth some investment. The commercial acumen of the gypsies is tuned to the need of the moment, and at some point, they travel the island with a lorry full of terracotta pots and palm trees. Some of these plants are three metres high and their large lorry resembles a mobile Kew gardens. However, these plants need water, and the public supply in the village is for drinking only. All private well supplies are extremely precious and piped water is very expensive. The piped water occasionally runs out, although that is rare these days. When this happens, only those people with large holding tanks have water available. A water ship comes in at regular intervals to alleviate the problem, but water is still a precious commodity. There is usually very heavy rain fall in the winter, and so much water is lost into the sea that some years ago, a large tank was built above the village to preserve some for the summer. Unfortunately, the valve on the side of the reservoir was not compatible with the connection for the pipe to the mains supply, and it took a few years to solve what was essentially a very simple problem. The water crisis and the gypsies' valuable stock of palm trees in the heat leaves them relying on the kind-heartedness and generosity of the islanders. The islanders tolerate the gypsies, as they do not cause any trouble. There is no point in them stealing anything, as there is nowhere to run to and they do supply goods at a reasonable price. They do, however, try everything to beg water. One day they claimed it was to mix the baby's milk, and given that the container held five gallons, I wouldn't like to meet that baby on a dark night in the crèche.

On one occasion, Nikos, one of the small taverna owners on the front, was watering his plants with a hosepipe. The gypsies must have smelt the fresh water from half a mile away and were there within seconds with their water containers. He had just finished watering and, being very generous, he lent them the still running hose with instructions to turn it off when they had filled their water bottles. It was like leaving a child in charge of a sweet shop, or a matelot in charge of a brewery. Nikos had walked off into the village, leaving his bar totally unattended. All they were interested in was the cool fresh water, it was too tempting to resist. There was mother, who was built more like a whaling ship than a whale, her diminutive husband and the three sons. She ordered the sons to strip to their pants and produced a very large scrubbing brush. Under the running water, she then proceeded to scrub them down until their previously sun-darkened bodies were pink and shiny. She ignored the screams of pain and the complaints until she was satisfied that their top halves, at least, were spotless. To the amazement of diners nearby, she then demanded that her boys strip completely and oversaw the scrubbing of their nether regions. Obviously they were very embarrassed about this performance, especially given the attention it was getting from those passing by. They did their best to do a rapid and discreet job, but mother was having none of it. 'More, more!' she screamed.

In due course, each was inspected and, to their relief, announced 'done' and allowed to dress again. They got dressed without the help of their parents; this was reasonable, as all three were well into their teens! That evening, they were all asleep in a row on the sand at the end of the beach like the contents of a sardine tin, all covered with one blanket. Four small humps and a very large one at the end. It was midnight and a disco had just started at a nearby taverna. Through bleary eyes, the four men saw group after group of mini skirted beauties passing by, and the lure was too much to resist. One by one, they got up and crept off to see the action. Normally their presence would not be welcome due to the pervading odour, but this evening was different, of course. Although they had no money to buy drinks, they were perfectly well accepted just standing there with their mouths wide open, ogling the action on the dance floor. All of a sudden one of them shouted out in pain and swung round to see the mother, blotting out the moonlight, brandishing a shoe. She may have been large, but she was pretty quick with hand weapons, managing to clout each of them at least once before they came to their senses. This apparently totally immoral activity of gawping at scantily clad and gyrating girls on the dance floor did not meet with her approval. They were escorted back to their sardine tin and ordered back to bed. After a while, the large hump of the whaling ship at the end started to sound its foghorn. One by one, the four smaller humps started to melt into the sand until all that could be seen was one large black mound, rising and falling in time with the waves lapping on the shore.

There is a very good fish restaurant, To Korali, in Ormos Aegialis. This restaurant never used to rely on the fluctuations of the local fish supplies, as the father used to do the fishing and the son looked after the restaurant. Some years ago, we saw father out fishing. He had a very small and classical wooden fishing boat that seemed as if it could only just accommodate the nets, but when he had his haul on board, it was really piled high and decidedly unstable. How it stayed afloat clearly defied the laws of science. The only place he could sit to row back to the harbour was on top of the whole caboodle. One evening he was still out until quite late, and there was some concern about the situation at the restaurant. Not necessarily for the welfare of father, but for the lack of supplies for the evening trade. The son was duly dispatched in a borrowed motorboat. When they found the father, there was no time to transfer the load, it was just a question of a salvage operation. Father was hooked up to the back of the motorboat and towed at high speed towards the starving customers. His little wooden boat had never gone so fast in its life. The bow was well out of the water and the stern just one inch above. Father hung on for grim death, perched on top of the mound of nets and fish. We didn't see him for some time after that.

Chapter XIX In Memorandum

We were taking advantage of a lull between clients to concentrate on putting together the following year's walking holiday product and developing our management-training programme. For the management training, we had to have very small walks to places where we could either run exercises, or use existing or planted intelligence for information gathering to solve scenario problems. One location we were working on was Astratios, a family chapel just outside Tholaria, which, like many gems on the island, most visitors fail to see. Inside this small and very basic chapel built on the site of an ancient rural settlement are just a few icons, and to the casual visitor very little more of interest. However, to the more inquisitive, a peek behind the screen hiding the altar reveals a fascinating altar support. There, in all its glory, is a Fifth Century BC Corinthian column-capital, almost certainly recycled from the nearby ancient city of Vigla. Next to the chapel is a ruined farmhouse, but closer investigation reveals that its foundation stones are much larger and of a different design than the rest of the house. It is, in fact, the remains of a square watchtower probably dating back to the Fourth Century AD. Most of these little churches have an ossuary alongside, which are traditionally used as family tombs. You can barely stand up in them and they are usually only a couple of metres wide and a few metres deep. Nowadays, some are used to store the paint tins, brushes and ladders for the regular upkeep of the more remote churches. Traditionally, the Greeks bury their dead very soon after death, because of the heat and the resultant unpleasant niff. In remote communities, this is normally done on their own grounds. Transporting a corpse slung across the back of a donkey into the nearest town, and then looking for the sheriff's office, is more reminiscent of a cowboy movie than rural Greece.

Some families have family graves, but usually only one, and after three years they dig up the body to vacate the grave for the next family member to pop their clogs. Presumably during that period, there is a moratorium on death. After the bones are dug up, they are brushed down and put into a box in the family or village ossuary. We were explaining this to clients at Astratios once and I went to show them the inside of the 'paint store', only to find it occupied by four piles of bones with a skull perched on top of each pile. They weren't blinking in the sunlight, but I'm sure one of them winked at me.

Ever since we moved to the island and the residents found out about our aeronautical backgrounds, many people have asked us about the possibility of an airport here. This is not something we approve of. It would be against everything we preach and practice. We are into preserving the environment and eco-tourism. Due to the mountainous terrain, the construction of even a short strip would be difficult. Also, the orientation of this long thin island is east – west. In the summer the Meltemi blows which is a northerly wind. Therefore a runway would have to be constructed north – south. The largest relatively flat piece of land on Amorgos is at the other end of the island from us, in an area known as Kato Meria (lower land). Just after the Second World War, the Americans were considering using the location for an airfield. It has also been looked at since. With a large amount of earth moving, and subject to favourable winds, you could land a small aircraft there. But there is absolutely no chance of it being capable of taking charter traffic without the sort of work that went into building the new Hong Kong International Airport.

We went up onto the surrounding hillsides to take photographs, for our survey, and came across the remains of a house clearance. The remnants of a few recently deceased goats in sacks drew our attention. Well, they would, wouldn't they? Investigating further, primarily because it had to be done, we found a rather sad collection of personal belongings. In a pile was one small rickety table, one small dilapidated wicker seat chair, a few old rugs, rusty pots and pans, a little well bucket, an old pulley from a boat and an old traditional glass lantern. The most poignant articles of all were the two diminutive crutches, which had undergone many repairs in their past. They were patched up with old pieces of wood, and rags wrapped around the arm pieces to make them more comfortable, which were very worn from the punishing rocky terrain they had assisted their owner across. We wondered if this was all there was to show for this person's life, but hoped that in such a small and close knit community, there would at least be many memories of him. Absolutely certain that no one would mind, or even notice, we liberated the glass lantern which, although cracked, is perfectly serviceable and will remind us of the very basic conditions that some of these islanders still live under.

The cattle from the farm in Agios Pavlos where we resided were let out of their shelter at night, when it is cooler to graze. These animals are most magnificent beasts with light brown coats, kind looking faces and impressive, but small horns. They are a Swiss breed of cattle, creating a scene more reminiscent of the The Sound of Music than Zorba the Greek. It is difficult to imagine Julie Andrews galloping through these mountains with the von Trapps, but the cattle make up for it. They are free to wander the whole area, finding what they can amongst all the dried grasses and flowers, which are all that remain in early summer of the spring flower display. There are only a very few Greek islands that can support the needs of this breed of cattle, so we are very lucky to be so privileged and not have to put up with any common old breed on our doorstep. A few weeks previous, we had some old bread that we threw to them in the field alongside our house. Gradually, they would come closer and closer until they were eating out of our hands. The problem we then had was that, as soon as they were released, it was like 'The Charge of the Light Brigade' as they headed down the hill for their Home Pride supper. One Friday night after they'd demolished a whole loaf, they refused to leave, and we had to eat dinner with eight big, brown, pleading eyes and four large, wet noses, just two metres from our patio. They then stayed there all night huffing and puffing and generally disturbing the peace, until they got their toast and marmalade for breakfast.

It was not unknown for the office to suddenly go dark and to turn around to find the window full of a very large head and horns. I was thinking of getting a hole cut in the shutters, so that the next time it happened I could close them and it would give the appearance of a mounted trophy on the office wall. However, it would probably be a bit messy for the computer screen if the thing sneezed or snorted.

There were also two donkeys that came to visit us, but their preference was apples. One of them got into our garden one morning and was eating all the figs on our colossal fig tree. Fortunately we managed to get him out before they took effect. The other regular nightly disturbance was four jet-black stray kittens. We had a fishing net stashed away behind a grape vine to protect our plants from the dreaded crickets in the spring. The kittens would pull this out and then use it as a trampoline, taking turns in bouncing off it onto the gravel. It is amazing how in the middle of the night a series of little kittens landing on gravel can sound like a man's footsteps outside the window. When they got bored of this game, they would play tiddly-winks on our bedroom roof with a pile of pebbles up there. I was told that they were cute, but they were getting dangerously big enough to barbeque.

Chapter XX Octopus

One morning we watched two fishermen at the bottom of our garden fishing for octopus (the Greek word, "octapothi," means eight legs). Some of the more intrepid younger men fish using snorkelling equipment and a spear gun, but the traditional method is to use a boat and a hook. The procedure involves two men, the rower and the fisher. To the uninitiated, it looks as if one man is rowing very slowly whilst the other one is being violently ill over the side into a bucket. In actual fact, this is a bucket that has had the bottom removed and replaced with glass. He is looking into it to spot the octopus in the sand at the bottom. When seen, a large, triple-pronged, unbaited fishing hook is used to snare it. It is a very skillful manoeuvre which requires precision and dexterity. The hook is dropped straight on top of the octopus in a way so that the hook embeds itself into the prey which is then hauled aboard. The octopus is then taken ashore and treated to a brutal beating. It is picked up time and time again and thrown as hard as possible onto the rocks. It appears that the fisherman is extremely angry with it or is trying to get it to talk. This action is in fact to extract all the ink from it prior to cooking. The octopus is long dead at this point and suffers no pain. It does, however, make you wonder whom the fisherman has got in mind when carrying out the procedure; is it his bank manager or mother-in-law? The fisherman that morning was Elias, this Greek name is derived from the Hebrew for Elijah, which means 'the Lord is my God.' Perhaps this is why he is renowned for his cool, calm and skillful manner when fishing, which may indicate that in some previous life he was a brain surgeon. A lot of fishing goes on here that involves a team of two, the fisherman and the rower. If it is the bucket and hook job, for octopus, the boat has to be manoeuvred into exactly the right position to drop the hook straight onto the octopus. If it is the straight line with a series of hooks and a weight, the technique is to put the weight on the bottom, and the rower in this case is given instructions as to which way to row to counteract currents and wind to keep the line exactly vertical. First and foremost, it requires a good line of communication between the fisher and the rower. Secondly, a system needs to be in place where there is an understanding between the players about what each sign, word or grunt means. Lastly, of course, a sound working relationship has to be developed which gives the synergistic properties of a cohesive and successful team leading to growth and prosperity for all. The problem is that there is a severe dearth of management development books in the dentist's waiting room here on the island and if it comes to that, there is a severe dearth of dentists. Elias doesn't need any strategic management books though, he has it down to a tee. He sits with his head in the bucket and back to the rower, just making the slightest of hand movements and waggling the occasional finger to indicate in which direction to row. It is poetry in motion and he always gets his prey.

Unfortunately this modus operandi is very rarely seen and it is usually 'pandemonium' in motion. With other teams it involves a lot of shouting and bawling as the fisher waves his arms, fists and sometimes even feet at the poor rower, who after a few minutes of this assault does not know if he is coming or going. The result is a perfect demonstration of how not to operate as a team. In a way, the control and communication required is very similar to a winch man in a helicopter talking the pilot down to picking up a load from the deck of a ship which is pitching and rolling in the high seas. The cool, calculated instructions and response are slightly different, though. Instead of the 'two port', 'three forward', 'three forward', 'one starboard', 'overhead', 'roger', 'three, two, one', 'on the deck captain … and winching now' 'OK to clear to the port', you would get very different commands. With these fishermen in the hot seat, it would all start very calm, but then get very nasty very quickly.

'Forward a bit, not that much, you idiot, now go right, no I didn't say it was right, I said go right, right, you stupid son of a rabid squid, OK, OK, my right then, what did you think I meant? What are you doing, you buffoon? You're going to hit the mast, stop there. OK hold it, winching down now, I said winching down, not go down, keep it still, you bloody moron, of course I could do better myself, no just stay in your seat, we agreed it was your turn to drive today. Oh my God, we've hooked the guard rail, no don't try and lift now, no, not 'lift now', I said don't lift now, stop going down, well you're flying it not me, what about the winch. It's on what, it's switched on, yes, Oh Christ, we're being pulled onto the deck…They don't make these rotor blades like they used to, do they? You'd have thought that they could have coped with that bit of superstructure and two funnels, wouldn't you? Have you got your bucket and hook with you, we could do a bit of fishing?

The postman did not normally deliver to us in Agios Pavlos, as we were too far off the beaten track. One evening, Dimitris the postman had a special letter for us and decided to make an exception. He arrived at our gate led by the landowner's ten year old daughter armed with a torch. He had negotiated two fields, three terraces, a herd of cattle and a dried riverbed to deliver said letter. It wasn't even a box of Milk Tray. He turned down our offer of beer or ouzo, but did accept a glass of water (he seemed to need it), and left with an assortment of UK stamps that we had been collecting for him. Dimitris had a van that made far-flung corners of the island a little tricky to get to, but his predecessor, who was a very large man with glasses, used to get around on a horse. He used to deliver to Agios Pavlos, and the lure of the clear blue water, especially on a hot day, was frequently too much for him. He didn't, of course, carry a swimming costume with him on his rounds, what postman does? So he would just strip off and dive in naked. Apparently it wasn't a very pretty sight; even his horse used to turn away.

At the beginning of August, our idyllic and quiet spot by the sea started to get busy with tourists. We returned from the village one afternoon to find a motorbike parked squarely in front of our gate, two metres away from the no parking sign. It had a lock on the front wheel that prevented us moving it even just a metre. This is quite typical of the arrogance of tourists from Athens, they treat the islanders with contempt and ignore all requests to make life easier for them. We added another lock alongside the existing one and attached a copy of the no parking sign to it, along with a business card with our mobile number on it, so they could discuss with us the terms of its release. An hour later, through the binoculars, we witnessed a very satisfying commotion. There was the usual jumping up and down, raised voices and running around, all witnessed by a gathering crowd. We awaited the phone call or more ranting and raving at our gate, but nothing. We then saw a pick-up truck with a bike in it, disappearing over the horizon. Inspecting the scene later, we found that the no parking sign had been ripped down and a large commercial wheelie bin had been jammed into the gateway to prevent access. We may have lost a lock, but it obviously got them where it hurt and was well worth the expense. They knew that their arrogance and disregard for others had got them deeply in the mire and they were not prepared to be told so face to face.

Our incident with locking the bike seemed to have had the desired effect. Apparently the miscreants stormed into the taverna opposite, ranting and raving, thinking that the owners were responsible for the 'wheel clamping'. The owners were then very unhappy with us, they said that 'we' were causing trouble. We put up another notice, only to find the following day that it had been ripped down again. To our knowledge, the only person that had been along there that morning was the grandmother from the taverna. Obviously the wrinkled little old lady, who was dressed entirely in black, thought that this was the greatest sport since they banned bear baiting over here in Amorgos. Needless to say, a car was parked across the entrance again that day, and we couldn't get out. Titi very kindly lent us her car, firstly because she is very generous, and secondly because I was threatening to kill the owner. Titi considered that the police might take this even more seriously than the claimed scratching of two motorbikes. Titi's car was something else. It was a small Fiat hatchback with the back seats permanently folded down. We had no idea what colour it was because it was totally covered in Amorgean dust, including the windscreen.

Some of the dust was thinner in places where over the years people had, with their fingers, written messages in it. One panel looked as if Titi herself might have used it to write a shopping list at some time. One headlamp was held in with sellotape, and there was no part of either bumper that had not been rearranged at some time or other. Some years later, Henri experienced Titi's parking techniques and realised the reason. The procedure being that you drive into a space between two parked cars until you hit the forward one, you reverse until you hit the one behind and keep repeating the procedure until the vehicle is somewhere near the kerb.

The inside of Titi's car was like the cataloguing rooms of all the London museums and art galleries thrown into one. To list the total inventory would take the rest of this book. There were lumps of rock, shells, pots, pans, oars, empty ouzo bottles (many), beer and water bottles, ropes, anchors, books, pictures and many cigarette packets, of course. And, this was just on the floor at the front and under the pedals. In the back, there were nets, string bags, a traffic cone, more lumps of rock, more empty bottles, buckets, spanners, fishing tackle, and floats and so it goes on. Fortunately, the vehicle blended into the surroundings with its camouflage of dust covering and no one could see in through the windows to see who was driving, so we maintained our street cred.

At 06.30 one Sunday morning, I bounced out of bed. The sun was shining as usual but the wind was not blowing which was unusual. I announced that it was a perfect morning to try our hand at fishing again. Not hearing a lot of response, I tried again. This time I got a grunt, which I took to mean, roughly translated, 'do you know what the bloody time is'? So I went on my own.

The last time we went early morning fishing, the fish were not hungry, but this time they were. They ate all the bait, but refused to hang around to come aboard for afters. This was particularly annoying, as our fisherman friend from Newcastle University had recommended that we use bottled prawns as bait. They were guaranteed to work, he said, and if not, we could always have them in an omelette. They were, of course, also jolly expensive. We have never dared to tell any of the local fishermen what we are using. They would be horrified, because you do not buy bait and certainly do not use something that you could eat yourself. After two hours, I got bored with sitting in the middle of the bay feeding the fish with our omelette filling and went home for breakfast (eggs, not prawn omelette and certainly not fish). We went across to a very remote beach on Nikouria Island for lunch (cheese salad, not fish) and afterward I went snorkelling. Around the corner, I found a lot of the little devils that had been stuffing their faces from my hooks earlier that day. I decided to have another go, and this time my assistant deigned to join me. Apparently 15.00 in the afternoon is a more civilised time to go fishing.

I had found an underwater archway in a promontory where they were all hanging out, presumably attending a seminar on the finer art of extracting bait from a hook whilst avoiding the subsequent invitation to a beach barbeque. We positioned the boat right above them, and this time it looked as if our luck was in. The water wasn't very deep and we could see them all start to circle the three baited hooks. As everyone knows, fish aren't really into afternoon tea, they are more breakfast and dinner people. But that day they did seem to be interested. We watched as one moved in. As we held our breath, it went for the bait, took it whole and then spat out the hook. We thought that this one was probably the lecturer from the seminar giving a demo, so we hung around. A student circled, and circled, and circled, closer this time, and closer, and closer and then, bang, he went for it. He took the head clean off the prawn and swam away with it leaving the tail on the hook.

Not so smart, we thought, still two hooks baited and still a lot of students to have a go. We were just waiting for the class dunce to strike when they all shot away. There was a commotion behind the boat. We looked back and were absolutely amazed; it was a seal. We knew there were some around, but had never seen one on the island before. It circled around the back of the inflatable and came up alongside. 'Kalimera', it said, well, of course it would, it was a Greek seal. Then we saw it had a spear gun. Now this was a worry, especially when we were far from the mainland in an inflatable boat. It rabbited something else and Henri said she didn't understand. Well, of course, she couldn't understand a seal, the dull woman. The seal then turned into a fluent English speaking Athenian in a wet suit. 'Any chance of a lift'? he said. I kept my head down, because for one, I wasn't sure if there were still any students down there ready to join us for a barbie, and for two, I didn't like the look of the spear gun. 'I'll ask my husband' said Henri. 'Tell him to bugger off' I said, 'can't he see we're fishing'? 'I've got two big fish here that I've speared that you can have if you want' said the seal. So we gave him a lift, and that was the first time we had ever gone out fishing on our own and returned with fish. We invited Titi around for dinner (fish, of course!).

One afternoon there was an eighty percent eclipse of the sun. Vasilis, who runs astronomy seminars on the island, got out all his kit. He had a large telescope set up so that people could look at the sun directly, through a filter, of course. He also set up a Heath Robinson affair involving a pair of binoculars, a paper screen and a piece of cardboard. This was actually very effective in projecting an image of the eclipse onto the paper so that everyone could see it. It could also be viewed from the bar without having to leave your beer unattended, which we thought was a very civilised way to watch the eclipse.

Chapter XXI A House of our own?

Late that summer we went to look at a house that was for sale in the remote village of Stroumbos. There are a total of twelve houses in Stroumbos, but at the time only four were renovated; the others were complete ruins. A fifth has now been rebuilt. It used to be called 'the village of twelve houses and thirteen ovens'. The story being, that with an extra oven no villager would ever go hungry. Stroumbos is a twenty minute walk from Langada, which is the nearest main village and road. From Langada, you first have to go down to the bottom of the Araklos gorge, which is the main torrent-bed of Aegiali. In the winter after heavy rain, it's sometimes impassable due to the deep water. But for most of the year it is full of flowering oleanders, and at the bottom under the olive trees can be found orchids in the spring. You then climb out of the gorge on a winding donkey path through the olive groves to the start of the village. The first two houses you pass between are renovated and covered in bougainvillea and vines. You then pass between a few ruins as you climb up through the village, passing a very small, almost stable sized, renovation on the right. Bearing right at the top of the village, you come to the house we were considering buying, with the fifth renovation a little further on. Upon entering the courtyard, you climb a few steps onto the patio. The view is stunning. Looking across the olive groves and the Araklos gorge, you can see the bay of Aegiali 100 metres below and various small islands spread across the clear blue sea beyond.

Many people that we have met claim that Amorgos is their favourite place in the world. Numerous people, including the islanders, say that Stroumbos is their favourite village on the island. This was probably the best house in Stroumbos, so logically, we were in some people's eyes looking at their most ideal house in the whole world. Having said that, many people would not live there given the difficult access and lack of facilities. The village has no mains electricity, water, or sewage, and although electricity has been planned for the village, we are strongly opposed to it because of the environmental and aesthetic damage that would be caused by the wires and poles. The house was renovated from a ruin ten years previously, but is between two hundred and three hundred years old. It took a team of six donkeys working six days a week for nine months to transport all the materials up there. The renovation was a labour of love for the Italian couple that owned it. They were both perfectionists and the final finish reflects this. All the old timbers had been faithfully restored and polished, and it had been very tastefully furnished with period pieces from the island. The whole lock, stock and barrel was included in the sale.

When the property fell into disrepair all the old roof timbers fell away, some were rescued and others obtained from other ruins. These beams are found in all the old cottages on the island. They look like twisted branches and trunks from trees, which is exactly what they are. The wood is called 'fithi', as in the Greek word for snake, because of its twisted property. It is actually juniper. The twist and the type of wood is extremely strong, and if you cut into the beams, that are hundreds of years old, you can still smell the wood as if it were freshly felled.

The forest where all these trees grew was in the region of this house on the Krikellos mountainside. Unfortunately, the whole forest burnt down in 1835 and only a few trees survived. The result of this is that any house with these beams has to be pre-1835. There were, of course, a few problems with living in this remote property, the first one being the small water storage tanks, the second being the concern about future development and, last but not least, the money. With care, and perhaps by joining the gypsies for the occasional scrub down on the seafront, we could probably manage with the water storage situation. There was expected to be a ban on development in Stroumbos issued very shortly, and the cost of renovating any of the remaining ruins would be so astronomical that expansion was unlikely. We made a few enquiries and everyone seemed to think that the price was about right. But we felt that more research was required before we could make a decision.

There were only a few more days of the peak season to go and then we could get back to normality. The busier it got down at Agios Pavlos, a house with no water or electricity, but a free hike thrown in, sounded more attractive every day. That day, not only did every idiot in Greece who owns a motorbike turn up, but all his or her slightly richer moronic counterparts with cars arrived as well. They didn't only block our gateway, they blocked each other in as well, and when the boats across to Nikouria finished running for the day, it was like a Chinese puzzle trying to extract them all. Still it provided us with some entertainment. At that time of year, peak season, there was an additional fishing boat taking tourists across to the island. They paid eight hundred drachmas return, but I would quite happily have taken them across in our little boat for free and never brought them back again. The weather had been extremely calm for a few days, and the weather 'experts' said it was the eclipse that had caused it. I couldn't find anything in my extensive meteorological library that helped with this theory. When it is calm it is of course very hot, and the afternoon has to be spent up to the neck in the sea. On such days, we usually took our boat to a point a kilometre down the coast, where there is a bay which the tourists can't get to unless they have a boat. We usually had a few yachts moored up opposite to us, but it is a bit much for their small tenders to get across the bay, so our beach had been safe so far. Not that day. No less than five motor yachts turned up, all with tenders the size of a small yacht. The biggest motor yacht was well over thirty metres long and the others not much smaller. Three of them all moored up together and then the crew got out all the 'big boys' toys and arranged them in a line behind this small flotilla. There were speed boats, windsurfer boards (not much use that day!), water ski equipment, a huge rubber ring that you sit in and get towed across the water giving you what would seem to be an unavoidable seventy knot enema. Perhaps rich swine like this sort of thing, as it's the only thing left for them to do. Small inflatables, big inflatables and of course the inevitable jet ski, which are in fact forbidden here, but who is going to argue with that much money! We got in our boat and disappeared over the horizon to a beach at the other end of the island, which is virtually invisible from the sea and extremely difficult to get to by land. By nightfall all but one super yacht had left, and all the morons with their motorbikes and cars had extracted themselves from their daily pickle and gone to annoy the shopkeepers and restaurant owners in the village. Peace was restored.

Being suckers for punishment, we popped into the village in the evening to take the pictures we had developed of the 'Eclipse Operation Centre' for Vasilis. It was mayhem. Not Rhodes or Corfu, because these people were mainly Greek and not British lager louts, and they weren't six deep on the street, but it was not what we were used to. Agiris was busy and stressed out in his shop, with people wanting mozzie repellent, before-sun lotion, after-sun lotion and bags of ice. Who sells ice? This is Agiris' little grocery shop, not the dinner party planning service department of Harrods. He was so occupied that he just glanced at our pile of goods and told us not to bother paying, we could reimburse him next time.

Paniotis from To Limani was there juggling arms full of watermelons and muttering about the number of days of bedlam left. They were all counting the days, but also counting their money! This grocery shop was very useful for To Limani, as it was right next door; in fact, when they were busy the tables outside went right past the front of the store. It is now closed due to a bizarre EU directive that says in this situation you cannot sell fresh fruit and vegetables from an area below street level. This area is the hub of the village and Paniotis, having the biggest restaurant, and the most buying power, usually has the pick of the fishermen's catch. It is a beautiful setting, with tables set out under the stars and flowering oleander trees where, surrounded by pots full of geraniums, you can watch the world go by. We have been sitting outside having dinner there on many occasions when a box of flapping fish has been thrown at our feet whilst the fisherman goes inside to negotiate a price.

On one occasion one of the old boys, Nikitas, came along the street pulling a fish which was about three metres long and a metre across. It was certainly the biggest fish we have ever seen in the area. He only has a small boat and it would have been impossible for him to have landed this in his vessel. He must have towed it behind, which would have been quite an achievement given his age and the fact that he doesn't even have an engine on his boat. He had a grin from ear to ear and was revelling in all the glory poured upon him by his rapidly growing entourage of colleagues. His boat was actually only a few metres away, but he had purposely dragged the fish with great effort through the whole length of the village parading his prize. He couldn't have looked more proud if he'd been walking through with a blonde international model on each arm. He stopped outside the grocery shop right by where we were sitting. Agiris came up the three steps from his shop to also admire the catch. It was all very well catching something this big, but the problem then was what to do with it. It would take Paniotis' wife a month to turn it into fish cakes and there was no fridge on the island big enough to keep it. It was reluctantly agreed that the only thing to do was to cut the prize in half on Agiris' doorstep. A large knife was produced and the operation began. A few people at nearby tables went a little pale and left, but we watched with interest. After 10 minutes it was clear that they were getting nowhere, so a large cleaver was produced from the restaurant. As they hacked away at it, chunks of fish were flying all over the place. All our clothes had to be washed that evening and Henri is still finding bits in her handbag to this day. All the time they were working on the fish, it was slithering around on the path, it was a real slippery critter. In their enthusiasm they hadn't noticed that it was getting closer and closer to Agiris doorway, and on the final blow, which separated the top half from the bottom, the whole tail shot down the steps into the shop and across the floor. It was only stopped from playing a very expensive game of skittles with all the liquor bottles by a strategically placed fridge. The inside of this fridge turned out to be the final resting place for this half anyway, so it was actually all quite convenient. Nikitas was now left with the top half of the fish, but no tail to tow it with, quite a quandary. A large bin bag was produced and the remaining fish was slid into it. He slung it over his shoulder and had hardly taken one pace before the weight became too much for the bag and the contents shot out of the bottom across the pavement and straight down the steps into the shop to join its other half. Everyone chased it down there and a few minutes later it was transported out in a stronger sack. Nikitas hobbled away down the street holding the bag over his shoulder with one hand, and his stick in the other, disappearing, literally, into the sunset.

Chapter XXII It's just a fridge

For the Greeks it is Tuesday the thirteenth that is considered to bring bad luck. However, our landlord Nikitas had inherited the belief in the Friday the thirteenth curse, presumably along with his British tenants. Our refrigerator was broken. The door had fallen off the freezer compartment a month or so previously, but we had decided that we could live with it. However now there was a constant hissing sound of escaping Freon and a plume of vapour which projected itself across the kitchen every time the freezer door fell off, which occurred every time the main fridge door was opened. Henri had got used to being hit on the head with the freezer door, but she refused to be sprayed in the face with Freon at the same time. I thought that she was being a bit unreasonable. I even tried to explain that we are on a very remote island in Greece, but to no avail. It was no surprise that the efficiency of the appliance was diminishing considerably. The milk had not been keeping so well and that day I noticed that the beer was not very cold. So that was it, life really could not continue like that! We informed Nikitas. There was little chance of it being fixed immediately, and we were due to depart in a little over a month and a half. So we needed a new one, and demanded it with menaces, or rather threatened to reduce the rent, a manoeuvre which always works. Electricians are in a minority on the island and vary in types and abilities, complex refrigerator repairs are unlikely to ever take place. A friend of ours on the island rented rooms for the summer, and as the electric sockets were virtually nonexistent she asked the landlord if some more could be fitted as part of the contract. Surprisingly he agreed and duly got in the electrician, albeit some months later. When he left, four more sockets were very neatly fitted around the rooms. However when she tried to use them, not a single one worked. The landlord was called, but as he couldn't get hold of the electrician, armed with a screwdriver, he did a bit of diagnostic work himself. Upon said investigation, none of the sockets seemed to be connected to the ring main or indeed have any wires behind them at all. When eventually cornered, the electrician claimed that he had only been asked to fit electric sockets, nothing had been said about connecting them up!

We were discussing the problems of buying property abroad with our friend Peter, who is Swedish and spends the summers on Amorgos. He said that it is not unknown to buy property and land and then to find that it comes inclusive with a donkey and the small print states that said animal has to be looked after for the rest of its days. The property we were considering had no land as such and only five rooms, so we said that we didn't need to worry about this aspect too much. Unfortunately there was more. A friend of his bought a small house in the next village, and after all the contracts were exchanged, hands shook and much rejoicing all round, they moved in. The first evening they were there, the front door opened and a little old lady walked in, proceeded straight past them and into their bedroom, closing the door behind her. It transpired that they had not bought all the rooms in the house. This particular room belonged to an aunt who had refused to move so, unnoticed by their lawyer, that room was left out of the contract and she came along with the furniture and fittings. It cost them considerably more capital and legal wrangling before they could persuade her to leave and have the whole house to themselves.

Following the complaint about the fridge, our landlord Nikitas was on the doorstep with two refrigerator engineers the following morning. This was absolutely amazing, it was less than twelve hours after he'd been told about the problem and our rent wasn't even due. As we rented two complete rooms, when we arrived we actually had a fridge in what was our kitchen and dining area and another one in the office cum bedroom. The latter was ideal for keeping cold water and other emergency items such as beer to cope with middle of the night thirst, but presented a problem in that it would wake us up when it kicked into life in the early hours of the morning. We used to unplug it before going to bed and then forget to switch it back on the following day. Titi's fridge didn't work when she arrived three months previously, so we lent this one to her. She was still awaiting repairs. Nikitas made sure we understood that if it hadn't been for our kind gesture of giving 'that woman' next door a fridge, we would have a spare one. 'That woman' was also a tenant of his, but they hadn't spoken for years, they just shouted at each other once a month on exactly the fifteenth day when he came for her rent. Regrettably my Greek was not good enough to explain that if he'd fixed the fridge of 'that woman' three months ago, we would have a spare one.

The workmen spread their tools out all over the kitchen floor, putting greasy spanners and wrenches in the middle of our previously clean carpet and set to work. I showed them the problem, pointing out the vapour stream in the freezer compartment. They switched off the power and turned the fridge around. Out came a blowtorch and they started to cut pipes around the pump. When they had enough bits of pipes hanging free to make a model of an octopus, they started to connect them up again. A huge pressure gauge was welded into one line and a pressurised tank of freezer agent into another. There were leaks all over the place, more welding was done, more hissing from the back. Yet more agent was pumped in and eventually all the pipes at the back seemed to be holding. They then sat on their haunches, bleeding in the agent a bit at a time, checking the big pressure gauge, wiping around the filthy pump with our clean dish cloth, which they had just commandeered, and feeling for a temperature change. The concentration, the cool and calm manner and the obviously well-rehearsed routine was like a team of scientists at a laboratory bench developing heavy water; it was all very impressive. There was absolute silence. No one even dared to breathe and you could have heard a cricket drop with just the two scientists at work and Nikitas, Henri and I looking on in awe. After a very long time, they disconnected the gauge and the tank of agent and stood up, with smiles all around. They turned the freezer around and proudly opened the door. We were very impressed. They then announced that it still wasn't working, but they knew what the problem was. They pointed to the jet of vapour still streaming out of the freezer compartment and nodded solemnly. Then they all left.

Later in the morning Nikitas appeared with a car body repair kit and proceeded to mix some filler compound. He splattered a bucket load of it over the leak and with the stroke of an artist applying oils to a canvas, gave it some finishing touches that left it looking like the surface of the very craggy mountains outside. It reminded me of when I used to make scenery for my model railway and I was wondering about the potential of setting up a small layout in the freezer compartment. 'Let it dry for two hours' he said, 'and at three o'clock the engineers will be back to re-pressurise the system'. Amazingly, at three o'clock precisely, they returned and we started to go through the laborious laboratory process all over again. We couldn't stand the tension any longer, so we went out in the boat to go swimming, calm our shattered nerves and drink warm beer. We returned some hours later to find the fridge back in place and turned on. The pump was running, there was no leak, but one small problem remained, it still didn't work. I sent off for a mail order train set.

We made a few enquires as to the professional abilities of the refrigerator engineer. He is known as 'Stephanos the

Freon' or 'Stephanos ten thousand'. It appears that the procedure he carried out on our appliance was, as demonstrated, well practiced. It was in fact the only procedure he ever carried out. If the fridge didn't work, he cut loads of pipes at the back, pumped in Freon, welded it up again and charged ten thousand drachmas regardless of the result. We told our landlord that it still didn't work; he said he would get them back. We threw it out of the back door and replaced it with a new one. The cost was deducted from the rent.

Years later we had a gas fridge. I am becoming quite an expert in repairing these units which shall be 'repaired only by a certified gas engineer'. I had a certificate of competency printed by the same chap in Bangkok who forged our friend Peter's driving licence. I am now in demand by a few friends who ask for assistance with their gas fridges.

Gas fridges have many uses: they keep beer cold, they produce ice for your gin and tonic, you can cool down wine in them and if there is any spare room, apparently, according to Henri, you can actually keep food in them. However, very few people realise that they also can be used for removing unwanted leg hair. I have no idea if this is listed in the instruction manual, as I do not read Serbo Croat, Russian, Chinese or Thai, and so specific instructions are required here in English. You go behind a gas fridge, wearing shorts, or naked if you wish, with a can of compressed air which contains alcohol in the propellant. Turn off the appliance. Next you remove the panel covering the jet and burner and blast everything with compressed air to clean out any debris. You then immediately ask someone to hit the ignite button on the front. There follows a huge flash and a bang. You then just rub off all the blackened burnt leg hair – fast and easy. Although, it is probably a good job I wasn't naked.

Chapter XXIII Perhaps we will have our own house

We had another meeting with the Italian couple, Ferruccio and Sonia, about their house in Stroumbos. They were a delightful couple and we were very likeminded in our ideas about the environment and the preservation of Amorgos. They were both tall and slim. Sonia had short, fair hair, and an extremely pleasant and serene disposition. Ferruccio was dark-haired with a neatly trimmed beard and, by contrast, an intense aura and some unconventional ideas.

They were prepared to take quite a reduction in their asking price, in exchange for being able to walk away with the cash at the end of their holiday and not have to come back to sort things out. They planned to go by air from Athens to Rome, so most things would stay as part of the proposed arrangement. By playing the currency exchange game, and with sterling being very strong at the time, we got them thinking about a price that was exactly thirty percent below their original Greek drachma asking price. We offered to pay in any currency, and told them that sterling was the best deal and far easier for us. We shook hands on it, shared a bottle of retsina, and the deal was done. We took to this delightful couple the moment we met them, and we knew that as far as the four of us were concerned, we had bought the house.

All we had to do then was to make it legal. All the deeds and papers were an absolute nightmare though, and it was going to cost quite a lot in lawyer's fees to sort them out. The papers were of course all in Greek, and as the house was up to three hundred years old, many were in ancient bureaucratic Greek. When Ferruccio and Sonia bought the ruin, foreigners were not allowed to own property in Greece, so they had had to nominate a friend to own it. It was theirs, but there was this complication in the ownership. The boundaries were originally defined by crossing donkey tracks and large fig and olive trees. The donkeys go a different way now, blast them, and old trees have died and been replaced by new ones in different positions. How dare they. There was purchase tax or 'stamp duty', as we know it, to pay. This is never done on the actual selling price, but instead at the lowest figure you think that the authorities will believe. For this purpose, even though it was a beautifully finished and immaculate property, it was described as a partially renovated ruin, with only roof and walls. These tax matters are dealt with in Naxos. The taxman, as mentioned, does come over on the ferry, involving a ten hour round-trip to check up on all the cafes and tavernas in town. However, he will not do this to check on just one house, especially when it involves ten hours on a ferry, a night in a hotel, a bus from the harbour (which out of season only runs twice a day), and then a forty minute round-trip on a donkey. Apparently even the lawyers get swindled, they also charge a percentage of the sales price for handling the sale. Typically the lawyers are quoted a figure that is half the actual price, and the balance is done in used notes and a handshake on the pavement outside the lawyers' office. They must get a real shock when they come to the island to buy a house themselves.

That morning there was a large gin palace parked in the bay in front of the hotel. I joked with Nikitas the hotel owner about 'his' yacht. During the ensuing banter, one of our clients arrived and I updated him on the conversation about Nikitas' yacht. Nikitas asked me what flag I thought it was flying, I said I thought it was Bermudian. A little later said client commented that he was surprised that Nikitas didn't know what flag was flying on his own yacht! The client was a derivatives trader and probably his mind didn't work at such a basic level.

We needed to get registered in Athens to purchase property. Under a new system over here, the property also has to be registered. This required the Italian couple, to go to Athens, so they very kindly agreed (in their own interests) to register us at the same time to save us the tedious trip. Unfortunately, more paperwork had to be obtained in order for them to do this by proxy. Another visit to the police! The police go into siesta mode at 13.00 and surface again to face any possible crime at 18.00. Ferruccio and I timed our visit to coincide with the end of this period at 18.30; the duty policeman was still in his pit. One of our friendly junior policemen (we share a birthday, but decades apart) appeared above us on the balcony, slightly bleary-eyed and wearing just his boxer shorts. Not a pretty sight. Some minutes later, he opened the door fully dressed in his uniform. We went up to his office, and there on the desk on top of all the paperwork was the paperwork with my personal details, including my passport number from our last visit. I wished that my office had such a slow administrative turnover to allow a document to remain on the top of a pile for so long.

Ferruccio produced his identity papers and I my passport. I then noticed to my horror that the passport I had proffered was my second one and not the one that I had given to him on my last visit. Trying to explain why I hold two passports would have been a nightmare and inevitably would have ended with me getting handcuffed and taken on a pub crawl of Naxos with my friend the chief. Not able to imagine a worse fate, I decided my best chance was diversionary tactics to keep his eyes from the paper at the top of his dusty in-tray. Have you ever tried to nonchalantly lean on a policeman's desk with your hand in his in-tray, while discussing a joint, totally impossible, birthday party in London? It's tricky. Fortunately his attention was totally taken up with putting inky squiggles all over the proxy form. With the concentration involved I expected to see a calligraphic masterpiece, not the eventual result, which resembled a chimpanzee's attempt to put pen to paper without getting too much ink on its feet. I signed it, the officer signed it, Ferruccio signed it, and then the officer signed it again. We are there, I thought, I was wrong. There were enough rubber stamps on the desk to re-tread a Pirelli F1 tyre. Every single one was picked up in turn and rejected. The drawer was opened and more rubber stamps shuffled. Eventually the right one was found and applied to the paper with the precision of a jet jockey selecting an Iraqi target. Then we started on the collection of relevant papers on the desk, working our way through them in a predetermined order. They had to be stamped top left, bottom right, halfway up of middle and very bottom left of the form. Next, came out a book of postage stamps. One fifty drachma stamp, two one hundred drachma stamps and two twenty five drachma stamps were torn out and applied to the form. Out came all the rubber stamps again and he repeated the Postman Pat routine, very carefully applying them all in the right order. How anyone can tell which rubber stamp is overlying another beats the shit out of me, but apparently it matters. Just when I thought we were there, he demanded money with menaces for all the stamps he had decorated the paper with. He had no change, and Ferruccio and I only had large denomination notes, so we left owing three hundred drachmas and promising to pay ('Trust me, officer'!) next time we met. The way our paths kept crossing, I felt that this was not going to be very long. Before we were even out of the square, the junior officer was back on the balcony in his shorts, quite clearly heading back to bed after an exhausting evening's duty.

It was Henri's birthday, 24th August, another year older, as gorgeous as ever, and 35 years old now. We mentioned to a few people that if they wished to partake in some birthday cake, we would be in Celini at 18.00. The cake had been ordered from the café Frou Frou some days earlier. We were quite taken aback by the response, all our clients turned up and insisted on buying us oceans of beer. All our friends from the island were there, including some who don't speak to each other, for reasons so far in the past, even they can no longer remember why they don't converse. They all brought presents, there were bunches of flowers from their gardens, candles, purses and vases. Titi brought an astounding piece of crochet work that she had been working on for months. Henri had never received so many presents. She was a little bit taken aback, but very much enjoyed being the centre of attention. There was wine, beer, raki, rum and brandy, but no cake, for some reason. Theodoros from Frou Frou knew nothing about it. He pointed to a chocolate cake that was for sale with two pieces remaining and asked if that would help. Not a lot, we replied. Fortunately Andrea, his Austrian wife, returned half an hour later and the most amazing piece of Viennese confectionary was extracted from its hiding place with a flourish. It was beautifully decorated and, as far as we could gather, consisted mainly of cream and chocolate. Her cakes are an art form. She had designed a birthday cake for one of the local fishermen some time previous that was a model of his boat, complete with nets made of spun sugar and little fish made from marzipan. After dinner we tested the old lady's staying power at her newly enhanced years, and at 02.00, we polished off a few cognacs to finish the evening. We returned to our house to find that the goats had been in the garden. Not only had they demolished what remained of our marrow plants after the cricket invasion, they had also meticulously pruned every one of our carefully tended geranium cuttings down to the ground. One of our two vines and all the grapes on it were gone and the tomato plants had been eaten, the fruit remained, but slightly trampled. Titi's garden had suffered a similar demise. Titi had been at Henri's little party and had got home 'tired and emotional'. She said that she had heard the goats in the garden, but instead of rushing out to get rid of them, she had found the 'music' from their little bells so soporific, helped by a gallon of ouzo, that she fell asleep.

We had to get up three hours later to take our clients to Megali Glifada, which was a walk they wanted to complete in the cool of the day before breakfast. Years of military training paid off and we appeared, on the surface at least, to be bright eyed and bushy tailed. Ten thirty saw us with a full day's work complete and we arrived at Celini just as they were opening for a breakfast beer. Needless to say, the afternoon wasn't very industrious.

It was a full moon and as a result, or so we were told, why it was blowing a gale. The Skopelitis had been stuck in Naxos for three days. There had been no post for a week and the shops were running out of supplies. More to the point, our clients that week were stuck on Amorgos. We managed to get them onto a later ship, book them into a hotel in Athens for the night, and organise for our agents there to meet them and rebook their flights for the following morning. It was a fairly chaotic morning to say the least. The only flight we could get for them the following day was early afternoon, and one of our clients was whinging because he didn't know what he was going to do for the whole morning. I had a few suggestions, but wasn't allowed to put them forward. In the end, some of our clients were, however, kind enough to e-mail us to say that they had arrived back in the UK safely and that the plans we had put into place for them worked. One of our delightful clients, Di Shaw, even sent us a little poem she had written on the way home:

Up early in the morning
Lacing up each boot;
Where will we go today?
What's Paul and Henri's route?
Don't forget the sunscreen, beer money, hat!
Don't think we're likely to forget all that.
An easy walk today -
Includes a Land Rover ride.
We'll take it slow says Henri
Rushing up the mountainside.
Sweat is dripping down my nose;
My feet slip on the stones;
Halfway up a Greek hillside's
No place to break your bones!
But now we're at the very top,
The sea stretched wide and blue;
The hot clear air, the smell of thyme,
The stunning cliff top view -
We won't forget the fun we had
Up each Amorgean hill,
Or the Amstel at Celini's
Which was (almost) better still.

Sonia and Ferruccio invited us over to familiarise ourselves with the subtleties of our new house. It is all about three hundred years old, with the exception of the bathroom, which is relatively new, and built to blend in with the old building. The purchase of this small area had given them significant problems some years earlier. Ownership of the land had been traced to a little old lady living in the next village of Langada. To transfer tenure, the three of them had to go to the Cyclades Land Registry office in Naxos. The lady insisted that they should pay for her ferry tickets and all meals for the journey. Also, because she was so old, she insisted on being accompanied by her young son of seventy-four, who also required the same subsistence arrangements for this epic voyage. They travelled on the old Skopelitis and quite rightly, the old lady didn't trust the culinary skills of the deck hands in a galley which resembled the food preparation area for the residents at a pig farm. She turned up for the expedition armed with a wicker basket brimming with cheese, bread, olives and figs to sustain her and the 'young' lad throughout the passage. We learnt a few days later that the 'Old Skop' had been sold to a company which had turned it into a floating restaurant on the Thames in London. We assume that the galley was going to be refitted, or at the least condemned. The thought of having to ferry that boat through the Bay of Biscay would make joining the foreign legion sound inviting. It is not difficult living in a house with no water and electricity, but Sonia and Ferruccio wanted to make sure we started off with all the best advice about how to adapt to these little challenges. Also, as everything was included in the sale, they wanted to show us what we had bought. They told us the history of the house and of all the antique furniture, and then we ran through the inventory. I got to do the tool boxes, paint store, outside storage areas and other boy's stuff with Ferruccio whilst the girlies did sewing boxes, kitchen cupboards and wardrobes. Basically, we were able to step through the door on day one and start living there without buying a thing. There was a library of about five hundred books, but unfortunately they were all in Italian. We were having enough trouble learning Greek and certainly did not have time to tackle Italian as well and so, regrettably, they had to go. I had been playing the game of 'I bet I know Amorgos better than you' with Ferruccio. At this stage we were probably about even, in that we both knew practically every hidden little secret of the island, but I didn't know how to get to a few places which he did and vice versa. One area that we did not know very well was the area directly behind our new house which includes a fascinating geological phenomena, so Ferruccio offered to take us there. We had heard about the large hole in the ground in that area but we weren't quite prepared for the scale of it. It is known locally as Vouno, which is actually the name of the peak just above it.

We walked north east for about an hour from Stroumbos along some goat tracks in a very remote area out towards the sea behind Theologos. An old farmhouse was the cue to branch off up a slope strewn with boulders. We couldn't see anything until we were right on the edge of the hole. To say it is a hole in the ground is an understatement. It is a huge chasm in the planet, almost perfectly cylindrical, about twenty metres across and a hundred metres deep. Leaning carefully over the edge, you can see down to the bottom where there is a flat bottom of stone and sand, with caverns leading off in every direction. Vouno has its own ecosystem, as the walls are damp and fertile and the air is cool. Creepers, plants and bushes grow all the way down the sides and it is full of birds circling around way below. The bird songs can be heard echoing around the pit, giving it the sound of an enormous enclosed aviary. Bees have built nests in the crevices, and some of the birds were migratory bee-eaters swooping around after their prey. The people of Langada used to collect the honey from these bees. They had a large wooden platform with many ropes attached to it. The men would stand evenly spaced around the hole, each holding one of the ropes, and would lower the platform down into the chasm. A few brave and trusting souls would stand on the platform and collect the honey from the nests as they descended. It was a very basic but functional elevator. It was advisable however, before alighting, to ensure that none of the lift operators had a grudge against you. Halfway down a hundred metre pit is a worrying time to hear a voice from above shouting down that he's known about you and his favourite goat for some time now. There are quite a number of bones at the bottom, but none seem to be human remains. Well not many anyway. We backed away from the edge very carefully so as not to add to the statistics. In some of the larger of the bushes around the edge are eagle's nests. These all seemed to be from the smaller Bonelli's Eagle, unique to this area. Ferruccio said that on one occasion in this vicinity , he had made a very rare sighting of an Imperial eagle with a wingspan in excess of two metres. Henri looked worried and started to pile rocks into her rucksack to increase her payload, should said eagle come back looking for a little snack to fly off with. On one occasion when we were there, an eagle and an owl lifted out of the hole and swept over our heads. We have even had an opera rehearsal there, thanks to a professional singer client from Boston. The acoustics are incredible. Further around the corner is a much smaller version of this chasm with caves leading off from it, and there is very little doubt that they are connected and would make a fascinating study for a potholing expedition. In the same area is a large quantity of crystalline rock. The goatherds and farmers used these rocks to make drinking troughs for their animals. The crystal is very easy to chip out to form large bowls. Many of these bowls were made hundreds of years ago and are still in use all around the island to this day.

Before we could complete the papers for our new house we had to go to Naxos to pay the purchase tax. We were told that the office was open from 08.00 until 12.00. There were three parts to the operation. Firstly we had to go to the bank to obtain the money, secondly we had to hand it over and finally we had to contact our lawyer there and give her some details from the various forms obtained during the course of action. We had hoped to carry all this out in one day, but as the return ship wasn't until the following day, we did have some flexibility. The ferry arrived in Amorgos two hours late. We got to the bank in Naxos at 11.00 to find a queue the length of the Great Wall of China. We hedged our bets and joined a line each. I won, but because of the amount of money we wanted on our Visa card, a telephone call was required, which all seemed to be too much trouble. Fortunately, however, when I eventually got close enough to see the cashier, she turned out to be the one that had been working in Amorgos as a trainee when we had gone through the painful process of opening our initial account. A few friendly words were exchanged, the telephone call was made and the cash was handed over. Whew! It was now 11.40. We had been told that everyone knew where the tax office was and we just had to ask the way from any passerby. The first two people had no idea; the third sent us to a taxi rank and the fourth to the taxidromeo (post office).

Eventually we found a policeman who pointed us in the right direction, and we arrived at 11.56 to find that the new opening times were until 12.30. We queued at the information desk and were told to go to room twelve, up the stairs. At desk one in room twelve was a lady who looked as if she had just been sucking a lemon and she had recently been told that her pet cat had been rearranged into a hearth rug by a raki swilling steam-roller driver. She muttered something about lunchtime, which we batted back with a comment about our return ferry being imminent, and waved a fist full of used drachma notes at her. She reluctantly proceeded to calculate the tax. The amount payable is dependent upon a number of parameters, including amenities, access, distance from the sea, size of land and property and the condition of the building. We told her that we had no road, no water, and no electricity, claimed and added that it was virtually a ruin and that we were a good one-hour's walk from the sea. She looked puzzled and asked why on earth we wanted to live there. She then made out that we were living in a mansion, virtually on the beach, close to a six-lane highway with our own nuclear power station, and easy access to an international airport. To support her case, we were taken to desk two in room twelve, where a map was produced which they claimed had originated from the military. It was in fact a very attractive poster with photographs of the island around it and actually had been produced by our new next-door neighbor, who is a professional photographer. If the military had used this map to plan a campaign on the island they would probably have ended up raiding Agiris' shop rather than the Special Forces headquarters. They claimed we were right next to Langada and wouldn't recognise the fact that there was a one hundred metre deep gorge between us and the village that takes 25 minutes to circumnavigate. We were then marched to desk three in room twelve and joined by the occupants of desks one and two. A lot of discussion in very high speed Greek took place after which it was decided that it was all way beyond their remit and a conference was required. Off they all went to room ten to see 'the officer'. They returned with a figure that was exactly the same one we had started with despite all our objections. It was now 12.29 and the cashier was about to close.

It was our turn now to be sent to room ten. 'The officer' was busy; we were allowed to take a rain check on this appointment and sent downstairs to administration window four. All the paperwork was checked and more issued. We arrived next to the cashier at window five, just as she was cashing up, but at the sight of a pile of used bank notes, she stopped and grabbed the dosh. She inspected every note, and kept turning them around until they all faced the same way, up and down, front and back, and were superimposed on each other precisely, before she counted out the total. The whole procedure took ten minutes. I had time to reflect upon the prospects of paying it all in one hundred drachma notes and calculated that it would have taken sixteen hours and forty minutes. A receipt was issued and then it was back upstairs to room ten for more signatures and then room twelve, desk three, for the final sign off. We finished the whole business by 12.50, twenty minutes after the offices had supposedly closed. Greek time can sometimes work in your favour. We phoned our lawyer, only to find that she had gone to a funeral. Expecting the worst, because it had been that kind of day, I inquired further, and managed to ascertain that it wasn't her own. I confirmed this by speaking to our lawyer later and giving her the details that she required.

Chapter XXIV The House is officially ours

A very special day; we had bought the finest house in Stroumbos, the most exquisite village on the island of Amorgos, the most beautiful place in the world.

We woke up in Naxos early, which was quite surprising after a very late night. Well, surprising to Henri after I kicked her out of bed and we went out walking. The old Venetian castle streets and the Temple of Apollo are quite spectacular in the early morning light and were empty whilst the tourists tried to gather together their befuddled, hungover single brain cells. The water was as calm as a bishop's pink gin and the air was still. The members of the Naxos mother's union early bathing team were out in the harbour in their white rubber swimming bonnets. Given the women's extremely sedate swimming style, their sole protrusions from the water could easily have been mistaken for anchorage buoys. They were in severe danger of being lassoed by a salty old red nosed yachtie and him tying up alongside. After the Seajet left at 12.00, it skimmed across the mirror-like water at about forty knots and banked into each turn, like a low flying aircraft. Just off the coast of Amorgos two schools of dolphins joined us to escort our vessel in, but unfortunately our speed too much, even for them.

The agreed hour for the house completion was 19.00 in Katapola. At the last meeting with the notary it had emerged that, as foreigners, we each had to appoint a lawyer and the lawyers had to be there in person for the handover. This was a bit tricky as there was actually only one lawyer on the island. Sonia and Ferruccio netted that one and we had to ship ours in from Naxos, thus the late hour, and the venue, which turned out to be the notary's house. The agreed initial rendezvous point with our lawyer was the bookshop; and it seemed more like a spy story than a house completion.

As we drove in, a cautious thirty minutes early, we spotted Sonia and Ferruccio at a taverna and joined them for a beer. At the appointed hour we approached the bookshop, four abreast, along the harbour front. We stood outside for ten minutes trying to look nonchalant and failing miserably. Eventually Ferruccio ventured inside and found just one potential customer thumbing through some books. Now the problem was that no one had given us a password or secret answer and response phrase such as, 'your mother tells me you have come out of the closet', 'I had to, her dresses in there didn't fit me anymore'. So he boldly approached her in plain song. 'Are you the lawyer from Naxos'? he asked, 'yes' she replied, and so we were five.

Back along the harbour, now five abreast, the cowboys strode with briefcases and handbags drawn. At the end of the village, we stopped by another taverna whilst our lawyer chatted up a young chap who was casually dressed in an open necked shirt and jeans. We didn't really think it was the time for her to be picking up young men, but fortunately we tolerated this apparent deviation from duty as it turned out to be the island lawyer. Now we were six. We carried on to the end of the village and up some steps to the house, where we were met at the door by the notary. Now we were seven. We were seated on her patio overlooking the harbour with the lights reflected on the still water and the smell of cooking wafting up from the restaurant below. It was difficult to believe that we were buying a house and when she announced that the proceedings would begin, we almost expected some Greek dancing, calamari and raki.

As we were not fluent in Greek, we were supposed to appoint an interpreter, but Sonia very kindly agreed to fulfill this role. With the two of us huddled together, it took an hour and a half to translate the eight paged contract in bureaucratic Greek. The lawyers looked bored, the notary served home-made ice cream and the Greek/English dictionary got completely worn out as it was passed from person to person in the search for the correct English phrase for the completely nonsensical words that had been used in this type of document since Socrates found he could write. For the last half hour, the young lawyer picked his nose and our lady punched buttons on her calculator and wrote out her invoices. A bible was produced and Sonia had to swear an oath that she had translated correctly. More official words were exchanged and I was a bit concerned, given the assembled congregation, that we had actually hit the wrong venue and I had mistakenly married Sonia, which actually would not have been undesirable. Ferruccio signed all the eight pages and six corrections, I signed all eight pages and six corrections, our lawyer extracted herself from the inner workings of the calculator and signed eight pages and six corrections, their lawyer extracted himself from the inner workings of his left nostril and signed eight pages and six corrections and the notary extracted herself from the inner workings of the ice cream machine and signed eight pages and six corrections. Finally the interpreter extracted herself from the inner workings of the English/Greek dictionary and signed eight pages and six corrections. There was much handshaking, congratulating, and everyone wishing us 'kalo riziko,' meaning 'have a good life,' and exchanging of keys; apparently we had bought a house. We paid the lawyers and I paid the notary, making sure to check that the ice cream was included; you can never be too careful. Then we left to have dinner with Sonia and Ferruccio in the taverna below. Much to our surprise, sitting at the table next to us was Jorgos, one of our new neighbours in Stroumbos. More than one and a half thousand people live on Amorgos, with only four houses in our new village - an hour's drive and twenty minutes walk away. To this day he swears it was a coincidence.

All of the completion papers having been signed, Sonia and Ferruccio left the island the following morning, in tears. They carried just a small rucksack each, leaving everything else behind in Stroumbos. We couldn't stay away from our new house any longer, we had to move in. We called in at the village for a few things and were amazed at how fast the jungle telegraph had operated. We had all kept very quiet about the transaction, to avoid rumours, speculators and embarrassment in case the deal failed to materialise. That morning we were stopped by practically everyone we knew and congratulated (kalo risiko!) on our purchase and then asked by a few less subtle souls how much we paid. The rumours on the amount have varied enormously from the absurdly low to the ridiculously high, and there are only four people in the world who are aware of the actual figure, although many claim that they know.

One of the few people who didn't speak to us on our way to our new house was Yannis. We have yet to see him speak to anyone, even his own brother Marcos, who owned Asteria, one of the main tavernas here. Yannis is an archetypal little old fisherman who is such a permanent feature of the village that he appears on many postcards. He was by then too old to go out to sea, but used to sit on a little wicker chair which was on permanent loan from Marcos, on the harbour front with his rod and line. He was often bare footed, but always dressed as if he was expecting snow, in an old woolly shirt, pullover and jacket, even if it was ninety degrees in the shade. We never saw him catch anything, and certainly not a cold, so the close proximity of Asteria and the food parcels from there must have sustained him. One time a tourist thought that the chair on the edge of the harbour close to the bus stop was for her benefit whilst she awaited the public chariot. It is amazing how a five foot, eighty year old can remove the chair from straight under the backside of a very surprised fifteen stone woman when he is tormented. Needless to say on that day, Newton's laws of motion were proven to be correct, yet again.

It hardly ever rains on Amorgos from the end of May through to the beginning of September, thus the water shortage. We were therefore not concerned about carrying everything from Langada for twenty minutes each way to our new house and leaving it all outside before returning with the next load. Then on the day of the move, it rained, and everything got wet. No electricity, no heating and no dry clothes; welcome home. The house is called Ελευθερία (Eleftheria) which means freedom. We didn't feel very free that day.

The first night in our new home was very peaceful. As the sun set, the sound of the birds was replaced by rustling in the tree by our patio. The previous owners had told us that mice lived in the tree, but we had assumed that there had been something lost in the translation. As it turned out, they were right, little field mice were running all through the branches. There are a fair number of rats around, so perhaps between them they had arranged that the mice would stick to the tree tops, while the rats had the run of the ground below. A donkey braying outside our window was the only disturbance of the night. Sound travels so well in the valley that this resulted in a donkey chorus throughout the three villages. There was also a puppy in Langada obviously missing its mother, as its pitiful howling also occasionally punctuated the peace of the night. The morning brought brilliant sunshine again, with no sign of the previous day's unseasonal rain clouds. An eagle was soaring high above the house and a flock of bee-eaters was chasing its prey in the most high speed and agile aerobatic sequence ever displayed. They were passing through the island as they migrated to the warmer climes to the south. We left the house to walk the twenty minutes to the Land Rover. We picked a few figs on the way and met two ladies who had been out collecting grapes in the cool of the morning and they gave us a bunch each. All in all, it was a very healthy breakfast and a good start to the day. But it wasn't to last long, because when we got to the Land Rover I discovered that I had left the ignition keys back at the house. I said that I would go back for them alone whilst Henri did some shopping. I was marching back off down the gorge when a little voice called after me, 'are you going to take these house keys with you'? Now I know why the locals just don't bother locking anything.

The rats, although very cute, can be a problem. They are small, grey field rats with dark engaging eyes. The technique that we use to keep them out of the house is to feed them near their nests, which usually ensures that they stay in their own small territory. Our patio is a few metres above the ground and they tend to congregate below that area. If we have any waste vegetable material such as potato peelings or carrot tops, it gets thrown down to them. They are particularly fond of spaghetti. They are also incredibly intelligent. They know that about seven o'clock in the morning is breakfast toast time. They sit down there on their hind legs begging for a scrap of toast. They prefer marmalade or jam rather than marmite. We do however get the occasional rogue who decides to pop into the house. These intruders are entirely fearless. Henri was sitting at the table one morning with our cat, Celini, on her knee and our dog, Amber, by her side, when Roland (or Rowena, Henri wasn't sure) walked in through the front door. He stopped by her, looked at the cat, looked at the dog and then just nonchalantly wandered out of the back door.

If a rat decides to take residence, it is trap time. We never use poison. Not only is it a very unpleasant death for the rat, but it could also poison any other animal that eats the dead rat. Many people do not realise that rats are very literate and have sweet smelling breath. We know this because they just love books and soap. They have an insatiable appetite for both. They can work their way through a book or a bar of soap in minutes. We had a phantom soap-muncher who just had to go. The trap was set in the bathroom. It is a humane trap which just captures them in a cage unhurt, and then we take them for a long walk and hope that they can't find their way back. They haven't found our GPS yet. When they go into the trap for the bait, a catch is triggered and the door slams shut. This usually comes down on their tail but doesn't hurt them. In the night you hear the clunk of the door and a short squeal and then all is quiet. You then wait until morning to go rat-walking. On this occasion there was a 'clunk' and then a squeal, but the squealing didn't stop. It just went on and on. Henri couldn't stand it anymore and went to investigate. She came back into the bedroom and started to put on her dressing gown. I said, 'what are you doing?'. She said, 'I am taking Roland for a walk'. I reasoned, 'but it is two o'clock in the morning and pitch-black out there'. She said, 'he is not happy so I am going to release him'. I went to investigate. 'Not happy', was an understatement. It was quite a large rat and definitely a Roland not a Rowena. He was just a little too large for the trap and two little spherical parts of his anatomy were trapped in the door. His eyes were out on stoppers. So, there we were at two in the morning, walking through the mountains in our slippers. All in a line was: Henri, me with a squealing and very unhappy Roland in the cage, and Celini and Amber, both of whom were absolutely fascinated with the 'prize'. What a scene. It was a good job that we didn't come across any nocturnal hikers. You have never seen a rat move so fast when we opened the door. Celini and Amber didn't stand a chance of catching him. He never came back, and probably never had any more children!

We were thinking of charging an entrance fee to our house, because everyone wanted to visit to see what 'the English' bought. Titi had already visited and put in two more bookings to bring friends. We had three visitors whilst we were actually moving in, and numerous others whom we missed when we were in transit. There is a big deep gorge between us and Langada which has to be traversed to reach us, the older local people are happy to do this during the day, but consider it dangerous at night, not because of the terrain, but due to the 'spirits' that abound! When you announce that you are going home after dark, they look upon you as if you are mad and when you turn your back to leave, they cross themselves and say a prayer for you. We felt we had never been so well blessed in our lives

At the house all the water is stored in two reservoirs that collect the winter rainfall and the fridge and cooker are run by bottled gas. Light is from oil lamps and in the summer heat is not needed although there is a small gas heater if required. Looking on the extremely positive side, this all means no bills for electricity, water, sewage, telephone, rent or even local tax at the moment. Private and public transport is by foot or donkey. Foot is free, donkey was the equivalent of two pounds return. Only a return 'fare' is available, as they have to take the donkey back, otherwise we would be knee deep in donkey droppings. Gas bottles have to be bought two at a time, as they are carried in panniers on either side of the donkey and just one would result in an unsafe load. We were berated by one of our neighbours for under-utilising the cargo space. Apparently a donkey can carry up to eighty kilograms and we should have loaded it up with other goods and certainly should not have sent it back empty. The latter is a heinous crime which is punishable by 10 days of donkey-train duty.

Chapter XXV The computer again

Yet again the computer had broken. I was using it on battery due to our lack of electricity and it suddenly died. There was no warning about low power, it just switched itself off without a controlled shutdown. We could not get into Windows or even get it to recognise the CD drive to reload. And, that meant back to Naxos. Up at 04.00 for a one hour drive to Katapola. The Hermes 'Express' to Naxos arrived at 08.30. After a quick breakfast we made the computer shop by 09.30. I had phoned the day before to check that the owner would be there to deal with our problem. He had said that he would be in at 10.00, but the afternoon would be better for him, whereupon I had decided to try a bit of begging to avoid yet another night in Naxos. On arrival we were told that he wasn't expected in today, I demanded that they telephone him, as we certainly weren't going to return tomorrow. He claimed that there had been some misunderstanding and that he had meant that he would be in at 10.00 at night, not in the morning. I blew a few gaskets and one of the 'lackeys' said that perhaps he could help. The new hydrofoil was running back to Amorgos at 11.30, and we dearly wanted to catch it, as the alternative arrived back at 03.00 in the morning. After an hour and a half we had Windows up and running, so we legged it. We just made the port in time and with this amazing (British) technology, we were back in Amorgos by 12.15. I got the computer back to our old house where there was power and reconfigured it for our mobile phone and e-mail. It didn't work. We were recounting our tale of woe to Titi, who said that she had a young man staying with her who was a computer technician and would we like him to have a look. Of course we agreed and Dimitris was produced. He was Greek, but worked in Germany. He was about 20 but, to us, looked more like a war refugee who had been marooned on a deserted island for ten years. He was barefoot, smelly and unshaven with long unkempt hair. He was only wearing some trousers which he had clearly stolen off a scarecrow, and appeared decidedly hung-over with a cigarette hanging out of his mouth. In desperation but under strict supervision I let him loose on the computer. He clearly knew far more about this box of tricks than me, but his befuddled brain wasn't functioning too well that day. I gave him a beer. That was a mistake and brought the whole proceedings to a halt. The following day he returned, well I think it was the same chap. He was shaven, washed, wearing clean trousers and quite perky. He worked away for a few more hours whilst I fed him beer again. His performance diminished rapidly. We were getting there, but his apparent low alcohol tolerance was bringing the little grey cells to a grinding halt again. He returned on the third day and finished the job. He was supposed to be on holiday of course, but he said that he had been getting bored anyway and enjoyed the challenge of working in the field without any of his diagnostic tools. It was all very good news for us, what a fine upstanding, smart, intelligent chap; I would never have thought otherwise!

Most families in a small village such as ours, which only had twelve houses, would each have their own chapel. These would usually be on a piece of their own land where they farmed crops, vegetables or grew olives, figs or grapes. Some of this produce would then be used to barter with. There are two reasons for so many chapels on the island. Firstly they are very religious people and like to have their own chapel close to where they work or live, often hours from the nearest village. Secondly the land was traditionally tax free if a chapel was built on it. Basically this is a very ancient tax fiddle. The chapel which is allegedly linked with our house is called Agios Panteleamon, basically the saint for everyone; very useful we thought. It is just a fifteen minute walk from our house, so we went to seek it out. Lovingly maintained, in a beautiful setting against a cliff face in a narrow, deep and fertile gorge, it has bougainvillea growing up the rocks behind it and three large cedar trees in a row in front. There used to be four, but one is now the main roof beam in our kitchen, which had been placed there when the house was restored. Inside are many icons and votives. These are small charms which are traditionally hung on icons, usually to help pray for ailments or health problems to be resolved. They depict the area of the body or the problem on a small pressed silver medallion. You see arms, legs, feet and babies. The votive of a baby usually indicates that the person is having difficulty conceiving and this charm is put up to pray to the saint of fertility, Paraskevis. If the lady subsequently gives birth, it is then expected that the child will be named after this saint. Paraskevi in Greek is Friday so these children are known as 'Friday's children'. On Amorgos there are many people of this name, so perhaps there is something in the water they do not know about or they are just too busy partying through the night to get involved with other things. We suspect the latter. Agiris' son in Tholaria is called Paraskevas as, many years ago, his wife Maria went to the other end of the island to pray for a child in the church of that name. In those days it was a three day trip. Her prayers were answered. Agiris still claims that he doesn't know if the birth of their son was due to her devotion or to the fact that she was away for three days.

Sometimes you will see votives of a boat or other objects that they are praying for help with. Traditionally families would have a whole collection of these charms, one for every occasion, and the appropriate one would be wheeled out and hung up as required. On our way back from the chapel we met a lady known to her guardians as DC or

Dotty Cousin. Our friend Anna inherited DC with her house. Anna arrived on the island from England twenty five years previous and was married to Michalis who was the shopkeeper, carpenter and barber in Langada. Anna had lived on the island for more than half her life, but to the uninitiated she appeared as if she had stepped out of the Home Counties only yesterday. She was a very bubbly blonde haired lady with a great sense of humour, which was certainly required to integrate with the islanders. When she arrived, none of the locals spoke English and she describes her Greek Language Conversion to have been the fast track method. It involved her mother in law screaming at her in Greek in the hope that the louder it was, the better she would understand it. At the end of every day she would go to bed with a pounding headache, poor Michalis! However they have got four children, all educated at the island high school, one of whom went on to Manchester University for her first degree and then to Salford for her Masters. This is indicative of the high level of education on Amorgos. When Anna and Michalis were looking for a house, they were offered one in the village with the proviso that they should look after a lady who already lived there who was simple. Thus, the acquisition of DC. DC was an elderly lady complete with beard and moustache but sans gnashers, she was however fortunate to be very well looked after. Her main job was to look after the family's two donkeys and take them to deliver goods from the shop to outlying villages, such as ours, which do not have roads. She could often be heard from one side of the valley to the next shouting at her donkeys, calling them every name under the sun. They didn't seem to take much notice, and if our long conversations with her were anything to go by, they probably didn't understand a word she said either. She was perfectly harmless and happy, but we were warned that whatever we did we were not to give her a drink of her favourite tipple. However she used to go to the back door of tavernas and ask for a drink. The owners had been told to only to give her soft drinks, but they felt sorry for her and said that they restricted her to just one glass. The trouble was that there are many tavernas, and many glasses later she would disappear and Michalis had to go out in the middle of the night into the mountains to find her. He usually did, under an olive tree asleep with her donkeys. We love donkeys and these animals are so well cared for on the island we wondered if their owners gave them names as they always just seem to refer to their donkey as 'the beast'. We have now learnt that they do in fact love their donkeys and secretly have names for them. They may call them Dominic or whatever when out of earshot, but they do not like to be seen being soft in public.

Chapter XXVI Life in a Remote Village

The water at our house in Stroumbos is collected off the flat roofs in the torrential rains of the winter and runs into two storage tanks underneath two patios. One of the tanks is actually the old bread oven and kitchen, which has been sealed up for this storage purpose. On top of each tank is a well cover, which, when opened will allow a bucket to be dropped down to lift up the water. This doesn't mean we don't have running water though. Traditionally all washing would be done outside, and for this purpose they still have small semi cylindrical tanks that fit onto the wall with a little brass tap at the bottom. This is called a 'vrisi' and is filled up from the well bucket. We have one of these in the bathroom and one over the sink in the kitchen. Showering, not something they encouraged of old, is done using a shower bag. This bag is filled with water in the morning and left in the sun all day to warm up. It is then hung up in the shower and water flows freely through the showerhead mounted beneath. On a very sunny day the water actually gets extremely hot using this system. With a water supply limited to waiting for the next rains, which only falls in the winter, one has to be very careful with water conservation. When showering, you stand in a large bowl and collect all the water which, along with all laundry water, is used to flush the loo. Any water used for cooking that is left over is used for washing up. That water subsequently goes onto the plants and shrubs around the patios and in the small garden. One small problem with the latter operation is that when the inevitable teaspoon gets left in the bottom of the bowl it gets thrown away with the water. When you realise that you are getting short of teaspoons you have to search around in all the terracotta pots and under shrubs to bring the kitchen inventory back into line. To someone living with piped water, mains drainage and a water heating system, this may sound quite a palaver. It actually takes very little time to adapt to this discipline and it is the way that the islanders have lived for thousands of years and many still do today. With the constant threat of water shortages in the UK, they could learn a lot from these people and their techniques.

We eventually broke the news to our old landlord, Nikitas in Agios Pavlos, that we had bought a house and would not require his again. He had of course heard the news on the grapevine, but he wasn't sure as we were still using the old house as an office because it had electricity. He went decidedly pale and had to sit down. This had not come at a good time for him. He had two daughters, both living in Athens. One had been married the previous May and the other was getting married in a few weeks. As a retired sea captain he held considerable status in Greece, and any wedding in the family was expected to be a lavish affair. These two weddings in one year may seem incredibly bad planning or a lack of his persuasive powers, but it had to be that year, which was 1999, or the marriages would have to be delayed until 2001. Year 2000 was a leap year and it is considered unlucky in Greece to get married in such a year. The result of this is that in the autumn prior to a leap year, the priests are run off their feet as everyone tries to cram their weddings in before the New Year. Practically every week at that time, groups of islanders were disappearing off the island to attend family weddings, either on other islands or in Athens.

At last the island was back to its normal self with most of the tourists well and truly back in their offices in Athens, and many of the tavernas and pensions were beginning to close. Also, sadly, many of our friends were going back to their winter jobs to earn some 'proper' money. Those who have private means or who had done well out of the very short tourist season had gone on holiday for the winter. Three of our friends who come under one or more of these brackets were off to Bali to recharge their batteries ready for the next spring. The extra police had left the island and the one or two left were now back in mufti and blending into the background. As recounted, we had some contact with the police that year but, 'I think', had a very good working relationship with them. In the height of the season when the Athenians bring their cars over here, they sometimes set up duty roadblocks to check on papers. Even though our tax disc fell off months previous, with foreign paperwork we came under the 'too difficult' bracket and always got waved through.

A few years later we were in one of our favourite tavernas when the mayor came in. There was a very heated discussion going on in very fast Greek, so we only caught some of it. Our ears pricked up when we heard our village, Stroumbos, mentioned. They had to be talking about us, as we were the only permanent residents there and people call us the Stroumbiani. The owner came across to us and said 'the mayor is warning everyone that the police from Naxos are here'. Obviously in January they had run out of things to do there. She said 'the mayor and the local policeman are advising no one to drive anywhere until they leave'. 'They are stopping all vehicles, checking papers, emergency equipment and vehicle conditions'. I can't imagine for one minute that all cars on the island carry the compulsory red triangle, a medical kit, a fire extinguisher and spare light bulbs. It was very good of them to warn us, because they know that our Land Rover and Peugeot are both illegal. They have British registrations and therefore can't be taxed here. They are very well maintained but do not have official annual checks. Strictly speaking, we should import them to Greece and register them here. It is a complicated and expensive procedure. Every year they say that the law will change in Europe and it will be easier to do and there will just be a small administrative charge. We are not holding our breath. We could see outside our friend Kolokotronis stopping all the cars in the village and passing on the news. The parking area was full and looked like a stock car starting block. Nobody was going anywhere. I went out and Kolokotronis said, 'have you heard'? I said 'yes our car is in a car park pretty well hidden, but I'm concerned about the Land Rover that is parked on the road. Perhaps I should hide it'? He said, 'don't touch it, it will be OK as long as you are not driving it. You will have to walk home, enjoy your walk'. So there it stayed. The problem was that we also had a friend's car with us that day. We knew that all her paperwork was correct, because she had been through the administrative mangle to achieve it. There was a broken rear light however, which incidentally was in the same condition for the recent service. I checked the boot and there was some emergency equipment, so we risked the short drive up to the car park. The Naxos police had moved to the other end of the island just in case someone there had not heard of their presence. The following day they were gone, presumably to pounce on another island for another 'no notice' raid.

Generally speaking, licensing laws for vehicles on the island are quite relaxed. Many people do not have driving licences, but in the summer the police do stop cars and motorbikes to check. They never stop us because they know we have both insurance and driving licences. However in the summer extra police are drafted in from Athens or Syros. These are rookies still under training and a little over zealous. They even stop the donkeys and goats. They fined someone some years ago for not wearing an almost unknown crash helmet. The fine for not wearing a seat belt is horrendous and this applies for every single person in the car who is not wearing one. The locals get used to these 'summer' checks and comply with the law. Recently a friend gave a little old lady a lift in the winter and asked if she would kindly put her seat belt on. The reply was, 'I thought they were only for the summer'. The motorbike and car hire companies, however, are very punctilious. For bikes they insist on issuing helmets. They also make you do a test circuit of the car park to ensure that you can drive a bike. We witnessed one 'test drive' where the potential client only managed to get across the road before he shot straight into a ditch. The bike and rider were both OK, but no hire took place. Another less fortunate couple we saw passed the 'test' but only got fifty yards, after hiring, before going straight under a stationary articulated lorry. Unfortunately the lady on the back was badly hurt.

A driving examiner comes from Athens once a year. He will give a little instruction and then a test. Given we have very few junctions, no traffic lights, only one roundabout and very little traffic, failures are rare. These newly qualified drivers are then qualified to drive in the middle of Athens. For motorbikes an examiner comes to Chora, where he gives a written test on the least read book in Greece; 'the Highway code'. You have to take your own bike, unlicensed of course. You then drive around some cones in the car park without falling off and you have passed. A friend of ours took this test and passed. Fourteen in all were participating. Only twelve passed, but it was very bad weather; pouring rain and high winds. The examiner said considering the conditions the two failures had driven to the test in, and survived, he would pass them anyway.

The island has not always been so lucky with such charming police, though. In the past the police posted to Amorgos have been very strange, lazy, short of a few brain cells or, in some cases, the only criminals on the island. It did seem as if they were sending their rejects hoping that they could forget about them in this crime free and remote location. Anna's husband, Michalis from Langada, the shopkeeper, barber, goatherd, musician, carpenter and donkey saddle-maker extraordinaire, was always very friendly with the police when much younger, as he used to cut their hair. His mother also used to cook and clean at the police station so, as a family, they were very well informed as to what was happening there, both officially and privately. He recalls one policeman called Themis who never removed his hat except of course to have his hair cut. This wasn't a long job, as he was almost completely bald and had an enormous complex about it, thus the hat. Some village wag had told him that the best way to restore a head of hair was to shave your entire head regularly and in time it would all grow back. Taking this advice hook, line and sinker, he would regularly go to Michalis for a head shave. For his daily face shave at the barbers his hat would stay firmly in place, but this more drastic procedure required the even more drastic, almost surgical, removal of 'the hat'. Michalis was of course sworn to secrecy and Themis provided his own razor, apparently for security reasons. Whilst this delicate operation was taking place, the door had to be locked and Michalis was not to speak to anyone who called from outside or knocked on the door. Now one must remember that this was decades ago and some points may have been embellished. Before the advent of television, telling stories of old around an oil lamp in the village cafeneion was the main source of entertainment. Being a kindly and tolerant man, Michalis feels sorry for people 'on the fringe' and tends to befriend them. It was for this reason that early one evening Themis turned up at his house and asked if there was somewhere he could hide. Michalis obliged and locked him in his kitchen, assuming that someone was out to take revenge upon him for some incident involving his police duties. During the course of the evening it transpired that the chief of police had rostered Themis to do a night patrol and he was scared stiff. This was purely because he was afraid of the dark, and in all his time in the police force had always managed to avoid said duty. Sometime later Michalis called to him as he passed by a cafeneion, 'Mr Themis, come in for a glass of wine'. For some reason the policeman took offence to this invitation and as he scurried away he may have overheard Michalis questioning his sanity with the others inside. This turned out to be a big mistake.

Later the same day, Michalis was sitting outside the cobblers when Themis passed by and asked him to accompany him to the barbers shop. Innocently assuming his professional services were required, as usual, Michalis obliged. As his back was turned to open the door he was hit on the head from behind and lost consciousness. A few hours later, when he recovered enough to walk, he went to the police station to report the incident to the chief. The only person there was Themis, who had locked himself inside. He told Michalis in no uncertain terms that he had a gun and if he didn't go away he would shoot him. Michalis eventually found the chief and reported everything. Even though his claims were backed up by others who had reported strange incidents, they could not get Themis to surrender. Despite these incidents he remained as a policeman on the island as if nothing had happened. One day however, it all came to a head (excuse the pun). Themis was sitting in a cafeneion nodding off to sleep when two ladies, Argiro and Eleftheria, were having a whispered conversation about him. History does not recall if it was about him being folically challenged, cerebrally deficient or metabolically inconvenienced, but whatever they said made him jump up and run out. Very early the next day he went to the police station and drew his gun and some ammunition. He went to the church and lit a candle and then proceeded, as policemen do, to Argiro's house. He knocked on the door which was answered not by her, whom he wanted to see, but by her husband. This shook him so much he ran away down the street to Eleftheria's. Here he had more success, as she answered the door herself, without saying a word he immediately pulled out his gun and shot her, then rushed off down the road. Fortunately she survived the attack, the bullet having gone through her arm and into her rib cage where it is apparently lodged to this day. He set off, on foot, into the mountains in the direction of the capital, Chora. He tried to steal a donkey just outside the village but failed, so he took himself down to the coast where he hid in a cave. Some days later his body was found there, with self-inflicted bullet wounds. The police force got a very good deal in the end, a pension for just a few bullets!

Chapter XXVII Monasteries

The Land Rover had a leaking clutch master cylinder. We had tried to get it fixed when we had no clients here, but instead the part had arrived right in the middle of our busiest time. The only person that was loosely responsible with spanners on the island at that time was Jorgos who, as mentioned earlier, was responsible for the car being off the road for nine months. I looked in our idiot's guide to Land Rover repairs and it said that a state school educated pregnant orangutan with three left arms could do it in one hour. Jorgos considered that he needed the vehicle for two, so we thought that we would risk it. We duly left it with him promising to pick up our pristine, but slightly wounded, Larry at lunchtime. When we returned it was nowhere to be seen. There were the usual piles of wrecks, pushed into the shrubs, which he had given up on due to them being difficult jobs like changing spark plugs or a tyre. I checked them all over very carefully just to be sure Larry wasn't there. There were a couple of cars who were, quite rightly, very nervously awaiting their operations, and a disgusting, filthy Land Rover with upholstery that looked as if it had been used to filter oil. You've guessed it, once I had wiped the number plate clean, it carried our registration. Fortunately there was a length of heavy chain close by which Henri managed to wrap around my ankles just in time to stop me from going orbital. I lifted approximately a metre off the ground, which wasn't bad given I was carrying about one ton of chain, and then went for him. He stood leaning with his hand on the window, about the only place not polluted with grime, his paw absolutely covered in black grease. He was completely unable to understand my concern and couldn't see a thing wrong with the vehicle and was upset that I was not congratulating him on what was, thankfully, one of his successful repairs.

We gave him an hour to put it right, saying that otherwise we would not pay. Very surprisingly we returned to a steam cleaned Land Rover and shampooed upholstery. The body work was almost up to the required specification and they had done the best they could with the seats, so we put it down to experience and handed over the money. Henri and I agreed that Amorgos is a very small community and it really wasn't worth upsetting people. Every day we advanced a little further on the learning curve of adjusting to a different way of life.

One day we took our clients to the Monastery of Hozoviotissa and, as mentioned before, visiting these religious places requires an element of decorum and respect. We do our best to instill this into our clients as we climb the many steps to this monastery which is built on the side of a cliff. However, the larger the group, the more rowdy they do tend to be. That week we had a group of thirteen. At the monastery, the men have to wear trousers and the ladies a dress or skirt. These garments are provided to put over the inevitable shorts and shirts worn in this climate. Unfortunately most of these items of clothing only fit where they touch and were designed by the Bob Geldof fashion house rather than that of Calvin Klein. They got dressed in the small vestibule and only saw themselves together looking like a comedy act when they reached the sacred centre, the main chapel. Expecting an outbreak of morale, I ushered them onto the balcony outside to avoid the piercing stare of one of the three monks whom we had christened as Papa Grumpy very early in our programme. My worst suspicions were confirmed, there was laughter and shouting which the compere of an Old Time Music Hall Show would be proud to receive. Unfortunately it could be heard inside. Papa Grumpy came flying out and demanded better behavior, but worse was to come. After they had been suitably chastised and quietly had their photographs taken, I stood by the door and escorted them back into the chapel. Grumpy stood there to ensure fair rules of play. Unfortunately during the rumpus and photo shoot Eve, a very lively and vivacious lady, had become unsuitably dressed by her skirt riding up and exposing her knees. Grumpy waved his hands around and shouted, something that sounded like, 'phone, phone'. Eve assumed that he thought that she was concealing a mobile phone on her person that could ring and break the silence. To pacify him she lifted the hem of her skirt to chest height, innocently trying to pacify him and show that she was not hiding anything on her normal clothing underneath. We were not quite sure if this made his day or he would have to banish himself for ten years to one of the establishments on the mainland where no ladies are allowed. Either way, we were glad that was our last visit for the year, with luck they would forget the whole incident, or failing that unlikely event, who they were with, by the spring.

They were all now in a very jovial mood, and as we began descending the steps, we passed the monastery loos and started to discuss the pros and cons of Greek plumbing. These loos are just holes in the ground which drop down nearly 300 metres to the sea, they do however have loo paper. The problem was how to classify these vastly varying establishments using some kind of benchmark that all could understand. Someone suggested that they should develop an 'Andrex Rating' quantified by roll points, 'Andrex' being a leading manufacturer of loo paper. A five roll rated loo would have a door, a lock, a seat, loo paper, soap and water. If any of these five categories were missing, it would go down one roll. The monastery loo had a door and paper and therefore it warranted a two-roll rating. It is amazing what idle intelligent minds can come up with on holiday.

After the last incident in a monastery with this group we should have known better, but we decided to take them up to one of our favourite places, the monastery of Theologos. Apart from festival days there is no one there, and therefore no concern over dress code or outbreaks of morale. We split into two groups, those who wanted to go just as far as the monastery, and those who wanted to carry on to Stavros. With such a large group it was inevitable that one or two would be unhappy about the precipitous nature of the Stavros section. Some others were getting tired as the holiday progressed and we pushed them to greater and greater achievements. Also, for some inexplicable reason, we had had more minor injuries with this group than any other group so far. It was decided that Henri would leave thirty minutes early with the intrepid high-speed group to do the longer walk, and befitting of my more senior years I would follow with my group at a very sedate pace. This voluntary split worked out at almost fifty-fifty. An exact split of a group of thirteen would have required Henri's surgical skills and would have resulted in problems with aircraft seats for their return journey. The result, of course, was that I got all the walking wounded.

As we set off into the mountains with the cloud settling down on the craggy tops, my bandaged group looked more like a scene from MASH rather than a walking holiday group. I kept listening out for the familiar sound of approaching helicopters and the distant cry over a tannoy shouting 'incoming wounded'. We eventually hobbled up to the monastery and, to my horror, Papa Spirithon the senior priest of the island was there, along with a work force of men. They were smartening up the monastery for the festival the following week. I had been building our clients up all week about the magnificent frescos and icons inside this incredible building, and here we all were unsuitably dressed in shorts.

Unlike Papa Grumpy, Papa Spirithon is very friendly and always cheerful, except when arguing with the chief of police on board a bucketing ferry, of course. He was wearing his working cassock and hat. He was completely covered in cement dust with most of his clerical garments tucked into the top of his trousers so that he didn't get it tangled in the workings of the wheelbarrow. Judging by the state of his apparel, this had happened a few times in the past. I decided to appeal to his better nature. I approached him as he was berating a volunteer painter who was apparently applying the green paint in some way that he didn't like. Before I could speak, he had a go at another poor chap who was mixing cement. There was no doubt who was in charge and they all either feared him or probably, more likely, who he represented. I started to have second thoughts about my request and tried to blend into the donkey train that had just arrived with further supplies. Just as I was pulling up the collar of my shirt to form two long ears and throwing a bag of cement over my back he noticed me. I explained the situation with abject apologies and he very kindly gave us permission to enter, the only thing he insisted on was that the ladies did not proceed beyond the screen. This was no problem as the frescos could be seen from the side. We had seen Henri's group heading up the mountain opposite us as we had approached the monastery and I had shouted across the valley to them to get a move on. I wondered how she had got on with this small diplomatic problem. Apparently she had gone through exactly the same rigmarole.

After we had looked around the church, Papa Spirithon invited us all to sit down and, breaking off his 'foreman' duties, brought out a large box of sweets. We all very politely took one each and thanked him profusely. He had also invited the donkey train driver, Petros, to join us. We had met him many times before in the mountains and, like DC, he is as happy as Larry but definitely a sandwich short of a picnic. This sort of job is ideal for these people because the donkeys always know where to go. When the box was offered to him, he beamed from ear to ear and a hand the size of a JCB digger went in and brought out most of the remaining contents. Papas just smiled and went back into the little kitchen at the side. He then went to the well and pulled out water for us all and carried on to produce some magnificent strong Greek coffee. Some of the girls are still trying to sue us to this day, as they now have to shave their chests every morning. Satisfied that all his guests were suitably catered for, he went on about his work, which was now to produce lunch for the workers. They have a large outdoor cooking area there that is used on festival days and he was utilising this to stew some goat. He had a very bloody mass of bits in a bowl that was splashing all over the place and was added to all the cement dust on his cassock to produce a very interesting pattern. It was when he decided to start work on the head that we all got worried about the islanders extraordinarily kind levels of hospitality and we were concerned about being invited to stay. We decided to make a move. We were surrounded by glasses, cups, jugs and coffee pots, and so decided, given all his effort, it would only be cricket to tidy up. We started to troop in and out of the little kitchen with all the wares. When he noticed, he started by requesting that we didn't help, but of course we insisted. He then started to get quite annoyed that we were helping but we were adamant, it was the least we could do. He then got very annoyed and pointed to green, boot sized footprints, leading from the newly painted wooden door step across the white, sun bleached, concrete path. Oops. Again, it was a good job it was our last group of the season.

The aim was for the two groups to meet up at the same time in Langada for lunch at Nikos' taverna, which is covered in bougainvillea with an excellent view over the bay from this mountain village. To enable this I needed to build in some delaying tactics. With a small diversion from track that actually made a more interesting route, I invited my small group to our new house for beer or squash. They didn't take much persuading, they were either fascinated to see this new acquisition of ours that they had been asking us about all week or just wanted a cold beer. It was probably the beer that swung it. They were suitably impressed, or at least very polite about it, and interested to hear about it being the former weaver's and cobbler's house. They were surprised that a house in such a small village had such high ceilings, so I explained that, in its time, Stroumbos was an affluent, self sufficient village and the 'cottages' they had seen in even more remote locations had low ceilings because they were owned by fairly poor families and indeed in Greek aren't even called cottages but stables and would quite often be shared with the animals. They loved the location and view, but couldn't quite get to grips with the fact that we live without water or electricity. They knew from their time on the island that many people still do, but here were professional people from Oxford living like this; incomprehensible! After we had walked the twenty minutes to Langada, a lady asked me if we did this every day. Thinking that there was no way she could cope with the truth that we sometimes do it three times a day, I said, 'not always, we sometimes get a helicopter'. She seemed happier then. Another man asked me four times how we got the Land Rover down the gorge and up to the house, I gave up with him in the end. As we hobbled up the street to Nikos' taverna, we saw the other group marching down, and both teams arrived smack on time. We never thought that all our Air Traffic Control and Royal flying experiences in the past would be put to such good use.

Chapter XXVIII Management Consultants

In late September, Tim and David, two management consultants who were helping us to set up a management-training programme on the island, arrived in Naxos. We met them there and planned to catch the 11.30 Jorgos Express on to Amorgos that day. This fitted in perfectly with the arrangements in hand for our holiday clients whom we had escorted from Amorgos to Naxos the day before and were booked onto the 11.00 Olympia to Athens. We could see them off and then get on our ferry back to Amorgos. Our clients were split between two hotels in the old part of Naxos Town. The previous day, on arrival, they had rejected the porter's assistance to carry their cases up the narrow winding steps on grounds of cost, a mere 500 drachmas for a large suitcase! At 10.30 Henri met her group at one hotel and I met the other one. My group had decided to see sense and ordered porters for the easier downhill section, having proved their stamina the night before on the way up. Having waited until all the bags had been moved, my group arrived on the quay, cool, calm and collected, slightly later than Henri's heaving, panting and sweating group each of who was albeit now 500 drachmas better off. I had left Tim and David sorting out their hotel bills and they planned to join us in time for our 11.30 departure. Walking down the quay I could see one large ferry already in, but it wasn't until we got much closer that I could see that it was the Jorgos Express. The ferries do sometimes hold at Naxos for a few hours so I wasn't overly concerned about this early arrival, but I asked Henri to go over and check if it was still planning to go on schedule, as there did seem to be a lot of loading going on. Henri wandered over and with great difficulty extracted the information from the port police that the ship had changed its departure time at 21.00 the previous night from 11.30 to 11.00.

Up until this point our clients had been very impressed with our laid back manner regarding the premature presence of our ferry, even though the nearest alternative might have been days later.

It was now 10.50 and Tim and David were, quite reasonably, nowhere to be seen. Bang went the laid back manner, I dropped my briefcase, jacket and façade and ran the full length of the quay, which is a good two hundred metres. I found my two colleagues settling down to a coffee on the front. 'Leaving, boat, our, run, now' I shouted, in a millisecond they had rearranged these words into a meaningful sentence; this is why they are management consultants. They made order out of chaos and then resorted to chaos themselves as they threw aside their chairs and their money in approximately the right direction of the waiter. They didn't wait to see who caught it and ran. Their suitcases were in a baggage storage area in the information centre next door. Fortunately this is a fairly open forum where all the bags are just in a pile in front of the counter. Forgoing the formalities of handing over tickets and gently extracting the bags under supervision, I shouted back to Tim, as I was two metres ahead, to identify his bags. He pointed at his luggage, a matching set of two black bags. He was carrying a large briefcase and the two bags balanced me perfectly so I just ran for it carrying both for him. David grabbed his bag and brought up the rear. To give them both their due, the most exercise they normally get is climbing in and out of cars and pushing a trolley around Waitrose, but they did run.

This would have all been hunky-dory if that was all that was required, but Tim also needed to communicate, and that required spare lung capacity which he just didn't have available at that moment in time. He took advantage of a one second stop to prevent us from being turned into three bright red rugs by a large lorry inconsiderately crossing our path as we negotiated the road. 'Mine, bags, those, isn't, one, of' he panted. Again all being in the same game, I worked out the code that we seemed to have adopted for this particular exercise, and in an instant threw the offending item back into the office. As we approached our bemused group at the end of the quay, I threw Tim's bag at him, grabbed my bags, jacket and wife and ran full tilt towards the ferry. Our modus operandi is normally to go around each of the group in turn, say fond farewells and wish them a pleasant journey. Modus didn't have time to operandi this time. It was a shouted and diminishing 'hope you had a nice holiday, got to dash, byeeeee...' It was 10.55 and we had about fifty metres to cover. The gate on the quay was now closed, but the port police opened it for us and we ran for the ramp of the ship. Four minutes to spare, but we now had the momentum and so continued at full tilt. Twenty metres to go and the ramp started to rise. The policeman shouted for them to hold the ramp, they ignored him. We stopped at the now rising ramp as they cast off one of the two hawsers, I shouted up at the officer controlling the operation from the stern. The bastard's reaction was to just raise his hands, cast off the second hawser and pull away four minutes early on a departure time which had been brought forward thirty minutes, late the previous night. These ferry companies do not deserve the business they get and bring an unfair disrespect to the whole Greek tourism industry. It really is about time the Greek government took action. We returned to our group a few minutes later, Tim's life returned to him a few hours later and we caught a flying dolphin that was fortunately running later that afternoon with Tim and David both on stretchers.

David and Tim could only stay on Amorgos for a few days. They were very keen to join me with the proposed training programme. They did however have reservations about the very short walks we had planned to some of the exercise areas in the mountains. Tim claimed that he was typical of what would be our average candidate, and he said that he found the physical aspect of the course particularly demanding. This is a very difficult aspect for us to grasp, because we did not believe that we were that much fitter than most, but perhaps we needed a rethink. It had been a very tiring two weeks running a holiday group and then immediately changing gear and adopting the mental agility required to talk about and develop a management training programme. The latter had taken up almost every minute of our waking day. It is probably for this reason that for the first time since being here we were both taken ill. There had been a very bad virus going around the island for the previous few weeks but we rarely succumb to these things. I suppose we were lucky that it had happened at the end and not in the middle of our programme and that it only affected us for two days each, other people had been sick for weeks.

Tim and David left mid-week, we were sick through to the weekend, and the following Tuesday we were due to get on a ferry and head back to the UK for the winter. Henri was due to start work in the Operating Theatres in Oxford and I was expected to open the UK office of our management consultancy company. If we had been ill any longer, we wouldn't have had a chance of packing up the boat and two houses in time to get on the Tuesday ferry. And we were both due to start work the following week.

Chapter XXIX Back to the UK

We spent most of the final two days carrying boxes of possessions between our old house in Agios Pavlos and Stroumbos. We were going to get a donkey train to help out, but in the end by careful planning we carried all of it ourselves. We were then in a position where everything that needed to go back to the UK was in Agios Pavlos, where we could nearly get the Land Rover all the way to the house. All our summer clothes and equipment, books and other items that were staying were in Stroumbos. All in all it was quite a logistical operation, not to mention the transportation and load management involved. As our place in Agios Pavlos consisted of two self contained units and we only needed one to store all our boxes, we had lent the other one to a young lady from the hotel. Kari was Norwegian but spoke practically every language apart from Double Dutch. She was absolutely delightful and had been a great help to us over the summer. It had been a very hard five months for her, but she had finished her contract and had a few days off with her friend David from England. We were planning to take the boat out of the water the previous day, but the two of them wanted to go and spend the night on the deserted island of Nikouria opposite to our old house and asked if I would take them. It took at least four people to get the boat out of the water, so a deal was struck. If they helped with the boat, I would take them across and pick them up the following day. It was a good deal for both parties. At tea time, I dropped them off on a sandy, uninhabited cove with clear blue sea and sky. When I asked David when they wanted to be picked up, he looked at Kari, a stunning blonde, and said 'Never'. I don't think he meant it. I waited until I was pulling away to tell them about the ghosts of lepers, man-eating goats and sand flies. 'Can you pick us up at 9.30 tomorrow?' he called back.

The following day, the 1st October, was the first day of the small mesh net fishing season. The fishermen had been busy repairing their nets on the harbour front for the previous month. This is actually good timing for them, as they only close their little pensions in September when the holiday season finishes. They were, however, very keen to get out there and scoop up all the small fish and squid that they could. The result of this was that they started at 04.00 in the morning. One of the best fishing grounds for this type of work is in the bay between Agios Pavlos and Nikouria, exactly where our boat was moored. When we arrived at 09.00 from Stroumbos, it was absolute mayhem. There were four boats working an area of about one square mile. Using the main fishing boat and a rowing boat, they lay out the net in a large circle with the top supported on the surface by hundreds of small floats. These floats (the same ones that Titi liked to dangle around her neck) are only about one centimetre diameter and so very difficult to see on the surface. Having trapped everything in this area, the fishermen then start to pull in one end to effectively close up the circle, and finally they pull the catch aboard. The circles are so big that in this small bay, between them they had effectively blocked any other boats from entering the area. I began to worry that Kari and David would be marooned.

Another potential problem we had was that, although they were unlikely to scoop up our boat, our anchor and chain extended at least ten metres beyond the boat into the bay and their nets touch the bottom. There was a great danger of them snarling up their nets on our anchor. This would have made us extremely unpopular, although we were perfectly within our rights to be anchored there. I decided to tackle the last problem first. I managed to pull a total of sixty kilograms of chain and anchor into the boat, along with various crustaceans that it had acquired over the summer. I reflected on the fact that this anchorage system was actually about the same weight as Henri; perhaps I should have put her down there for the summer and saved on the cost of all that chain! We managed to land it and then looked at the state of the inside of the boat, which I had spent the whole previous day cleaning. What a mess! I had promised to pick them up at 09.30 and it was now 09.25. I glanced across the water and noticed that two of the boats were at the stage of pulling in their nets, and there was a channel I could navigate through. Henri stayed at Agios Pavlos, in case I got marooned over there as well, and I went for it. Very slowly at first, trying to pick out the small floats on the surface, but when I got across to the first bay of Nikouria I was safe. They were in the third bay along, so I just had to stay close to the shore. It was 09.27 and I was determined to impress them with the punctuality for which we now have a reputation on the island. I opened the throttle and with a small fuel load and just one person, it motored. I thought I would surprise them by appearing out of the blue (sea and sky) by hugging the headland and powering into the bay at about thirty knots. They were certainly surprised; they were standing on the beach stark naked. Pandemonium ensued as I cut the throttle, lifted the engine and hit the beach smack on 9.30. I stood there grinning, 'you should have known I'd be on time', I said. Apparently they didn't have a watch with them, so all my effort had gone to waste. Whilst they got their act together I walked along the beach. It was strewn with lots of small dead fish that had been caught in the nets but had fallen out before they could be hauled aboard. Many were the species that we had spent all those hours fishing for. We would have been delighted with a haul like that, but these were effectively the wastage. This was a very small scale operation, I reflected on the fish that must be lost in the North

Sea every day. I inspected my two passengers and announced them now suitably dressed to be taken back into civilisation.

We just managed to get back across before the nets closed up the bay again. Getting the boat out of the water was just as difficult as we had imagined. We took the engine off first and carried it up to the house for cleaning. The problem with the boat was that the track between the thorn bushes up to the house is narrower than the boat and with two people on either side, one couple was always going to get scratched. Thanks to Kari and David we made it but it involved substantial blood loss on all sides. We then spent two hours flushing the engine through and washing down the inflatable, dismantling it and collapsing it. Once it was all loaded into the Land Rover, we took it to the hotel where it was being stored for the winter. Nikitas, the owner, is more practical than his wife Ireni, and he said that if it went into a cellar room the mice would chew the rubber, so he suggested we put it into one of the bedrooms as they would now be free until the spring. The engine was left lying on a bed, sixty kilograms of chain and anchor alongside and one big eight-man inflatable jammed against the dressing table. If Ireni ever found out she would go crazy.

We spent the afternoon closing up the house in Stroumbos. I had been left with a check list written by Ferruccio, but as it was in Italian it was about much use as a chocolate teapot. However, such was their organisation that whichever way we turned there was an implement, catch, shutter or whatever was required for every eventuality. With the skylights secure, shutters in place, overflow pipes fitted, gas bottles turned off and doors locked, it was time to leave. We had only been living there for one month, but it was a real wrench leaving. We could now understand why Sonia and Ferruccio were so upset when they left. They had spent two years renovating the house and eight years living there. The next task was to try to get all the office equipment and boxes going back to the UK from Agios Pavlos into the Land Rover. With the boat and engine staying, this turned out to be a very easy task. The only thing that slowed us down was Titi's inherent kindness and the impression that anyone engaged in this sort of activity has to be liberally lubricated with copious amounts of ouzo. Now came the difficult bit, which was to go into the port of Aegiali and say goodbye to all our friends. We took Titi out for dinner and sat at a table in the middle of the village. By the time we had finished, we had collected so many hangers-on that we had to move to Celini. Round after round of drinks were bought and the Land Rover found its way back to Agios Pavlos where we spent the night.

Titi wanted to come to the port with us, so we went next door to get her at 08.00. Three large ouzos were poured for breakfast, well it is a kind of fruit juice and then we drove to the port. Historically, the ship ran an hour late, so we sat down with the harbour master, who insisted on buying us a breakfast beer. We had known the harbour master for years, but apart from a few pleasantries we had never spoken to her at length before. At the larger ports people holding this post get a uniform, but not at the smaller ones. Aegiali must hold some importance in the authorities eyes, as she did at least have a uniform peaked cap. On the quay we said goodbye to Agiris the grocer, Socrates the doctor, Michalis from Langada, Lefteris the shipping agent and of course Titi. We had barely got the Land Rover onto the ramp when the ship pulled away. By the time we had manoeuvred the vehicle on the car deck to the required position and got onto deck, the quay could hardly be seen.

This however was not the end of Amorgos and our friends until the following year, because on board with us was our English friend Anna, Jorgos our next door neighbour from Stroumbos, a few other people we knew from the village but most importantly, Papa Spirithon, who held forth to various people for the whole journey. This was an epic performance that any speaker at Hyde Park corner would be proud of, given that sailing to Athens took eleven hours. As it was one of the few ferries of the week in those days, it called in at every small island it could find. As the ship approached Athens, we said goodbye to everyone including Papas, who fortunately seemed to have forgotten the wet paint incident. The ferry docked and the ramp opened. There was Piraeus at its worst. It was a very busy night. There were traffic lights, zebra crossings, traffic jams, and people all over the road, policemen blowing their whistles, cars hooting their horns, exhaust fumes everywhere and not a donkey or goat in sight. I was tempted to put Larry into reverse and back onto the ferry to go back to Amorgos. Despite my rising desire to return we were just swept along with the rest of the traffic into the centre of the city. This isn't exactly where we wanted to be, as we were intending to head out to the west to the port of Patras in the Peloponnese. I was taking no prisoners though. I just aimed the iron girder of a front bumper with one and a half tonnes of Land Rover behind it in the direction instructed by my navigator, and everyone got out of our way again. Then 'Henri the Navigator' said. 'I don't know where we are'. This is not what I wanted to hear. I said, 'but you have been following the map haven't you?'. 'Well not exactly', she said, 'I have been following road signs'. I said, 'I could do that. The whole reason for you having a map is to follow that, not the bloody road signs'. After a short committee meeting at a set of traffic lights, we changed roles. Henri hadn't driven for six months, had never driven on the continent and had only a few hours experience of this very difficult vehicle. A recipe for disaster you may think; wrong, it was a case of needs must. I leapt out a few times to ask directions and in the end a very kind taxi driver said, 'I am going that way just follow me'. We got on the road to Patras without a single scratch on Larry. Mind you, we didn't look behind to see if we'd left a trail of destruction. An hour later we were at Kineta beach just outside Corinth, where we spent the night.

From Patras we took the ferry to Ancona in Italy and drove on to Parma, where we stayed in the same hotel as we had on the way down. If the weather was nice, we were going to take that day at a leisurely pace and possibly stop off for the afternoon and night in the Alps. Overnight there had been a horrendous thunderstorm right overhead that had kept us awake. The morning however was clear and we had a wonderful drive through the Alps on relatively traffic free toll roads. By early afternoon, we reached our intended destination in the French Alps. To us the rest of the day would have seemed wasted if we stopped then. We had got to the stage where we just wanted to get home. So we pushed on to just north of Dijon, where we stayed in a very comfortable motel and I promised Henri a nice meal in their homely looking dining room and bar. I said that you can't go wrong in France, their food is always excellent. I was wrong and it's not easy to mess up a peppered steak, but this chef did.

The following morning we woke up to clear skies and a frost on the Land Rover. First the traffic in Athens and now frost, welcome back to reality. We hit the road early, yet again intending to take it slowly and stay the night around Calais. We made Calais by early afternoon, so we did the hypermarkets. We tried to fill up with cheap diesel, but the pump just kept on shouting at me in French, so I told it where to put itself in Greek and left the filler cap with it in my frustration. We headed for the channel tunnel and got on the first departing train when a sharp-eyed guard chappie spotted the lack of filler cap. Fortunately we were just about to set off, so he was very reasonable about it. He stood there bemused as I jammed a rolled-up copy of the Financial Times in the hole (there's yet another use for this prestigious newspaper) and added a plastic bag on top. I think we were lucky he was French, as his 'jobs-worthy' English counterpart probably wouldn't have been so understanding. He then spent the rest of the thirty-minute journey walking up and down our compartment logging a squeak from underneath the floor. He confided in me that it was a fault on the emergency breaking system and that if we needed to stop in a hurry we might not be able to. We just kept our fingers crossed that there weren't any fish on the line.

In the airlines business, even if all four engines have fallen off, you reassure your passengers in a cool and calm manner that it is all a perfectly normal operating procedure and only admit that something is wrong when you are sitting in a smoking heap off the end of the runway. Apparently that is not how it works at Eurotunnel, which is nevertheless a great service. We were out on the UK motorway system as soon as they managed to un-jam a coach with a rookie driver from the doorway two buses ahead of us. We were back in Oxford by eight o'clock in the evening. Thirty one hours on ferries, thirty one hours driving and forty five minutes on a train. Mainland Greece to the UK in exactly three days again.

Chapter XXX Winters in the UK

It takes some time to readjust to life away from the island. Apparently you need to carry money with you. Waitrose will not let you pay next week. The smaller shops and bars don't like you helping yourself off the shelves and just walking out. You have to show a tax disc on your vehicle and carry papers for the car. You can't fall out of a bar into your Land Rover and then expect the policeman waiting for you to join you for another drink. You can't merely park in the middle of the road and expect people to just wait for you to return without offering derogatory remarks about your parentage. You don't stop every time you see another car coming the other way and expect him to stop for a chat. You can't just leave your shopping in the street whilst you pop in to have lunch with friends without people thinking it is a charitable handout. You cannot leave your wallet on a wall with a stone on it and expect it to be still there two days later when you return. You are considered a little odd if you greet everyone you pass in Oxford Street with a cheery hello. You never get home to find piles of donated groceries and the odd fish or lump of lamb on your doorstep. The manager of Waitrose doesn't throw you cartons of milk from his car as he passes and he doesn't force you to drink rocket fuel at nine o'clock in the morning, although this may be a blessing.

You can, however, turn on a tap and get water out of it and expect electricity and telephones to be connected to your house. You can drive right up to your home and don't need to hire a donkey to deliver heavy goods. You don't expect the doctor to discuss your ailments and potential remedies with all and sundry at your local pub. You can get to a dentist, optician, or vet without spending two days on a boat in a force eight gale. You can have television programmes beamed right into your sitting room so that you can fester in front of some Australian soap opera every evening and develop a lovely thrombosis in every artery of your body. You can have the post delivered to your door daily and find piles of bills on the doormat to worry about and give you high blood pressure. You can also get stuck in traffic jams and experience or practice road rage and stress. You can sit at a comfortable desk and work a forty-hour week; trapped in an office in a noisy polluted city. You can eat food that, if you are lucky, only contains about twenty different chemicals. Best of all you can work in the city all your life and expect a pension when you retire, wondering why the actuary has been so generous with the returns. There is life and then there is 'Life'. It didn't take long for us to realize that we had only one course to follow, and that was a donkey track leading: 'Out of the Rat Race Back into the Fire'.

Our Welsh Border Collie, Amber, was one of the first in the UK to get a pet passport. She was a pedigree red and had all the traits of your typical Border Collie. Stubborn, but incredibly intelligent, curious and extremely energetic. She had had to stay in the UK in 1999, but in March 2000 it was decided that I should drive the Land Rover across Europe with her and Henri would fly and join us on Amorgos a week later. I arrived at French customs with Amber, passport in mouth and microchip in neck. There had been many scare stories about malfunctioning chips and French bureaucracy. We approached the post with trepidation, convinced that Amber could charm her way through. I didn't count on her being racist though, and at the first sight of a Frenchman, she went ballistic. She was snarling, snapping and generally threatening to start another Waterloo, and this was to a person who was supposed to approach her with a scanner to verify that the chip agreed with the passport. As I dragged her out of the Land Rover, her territorial outburst seemed to settle and she decided that France wasn't so bad after all. She also decided that the interest the French authorities had taken in her was actually quite fun and now wanted to play. At four o'clock in the morning and with nothing else to do, the officers were quite happy to oblige and reciprocate with this newfound type of import. The next job was to see if they remembered their training in using their new scanner. Every one of them had to see if they could use it and identify Amber's chip. All succeeded and with smiles all around, we drove through the post and entered the 'continent'. It was only half an hour later that I realised that no one had asked to see the 'pet passport' to confirm it was the right dog with the necessary immunisations.

Apart from an oil leak in mid France which resulted in both the dog and myself getting covered in black gunge, all went well. We also made much better progress without the navigator present whinging about stopping for a coffee, lunch, dinner, sleep, the ladies, etc. Amber was quite happy just watching the French and Italian countryside roll by, enjoying sniffing new smells at fuel stops, and playing in the snow in the Alps.

On the ferry from Ancona to Greece dogs are consigned to kennels on the deck whilst human passengers enjoy the luxuries of these superb Superfast Ferries. When we were escorted to my cabin so I could store my luggage, Amber seemed to have a premonition about the impending 18-hour imprisonment. She dived under one of the low bunks and refused to budge. No bribery, threats, shouts, dragging and poking would shift her. So there she stayed for 18 hours with a bowl of water and the occasional biscuit thrown under. I'd explained to her before we boarded the need to visit the little dog's room, but despite walking her up and down on the quay in Italy, she had refused to perform. As a result, I calculated upon our arrival in Greece, she had gone 30 hours without relieving herself. As soon as we came off the ramp in Patras, I shot across the road and threw her out of the Land Rover. The result of her extended incarceration and self-imposed abstinence had to be treated as a roundabout for the rest of the summer.

The drive from Patras, the port of arrival in Greece, to the port of Piraeus, near Athens, takes about three and a half hours. Our first available ferry from Piraeus to Naxos was in three and a half hours' time. Not a hope in hell, I thought. However, as we approached Athens it was becoming more apparent that we could make it. I was pushing the Land Rover to its limits, and going downhill with a following wind at one point we nearly touched 65 kilometres per hour and the sound of the engine and tyres were deafening. Approaching Athens with 15 minutes left, I was very conscious that one wrong turn could result in a two day wait on the quay for the next ship. Anyone who has driven in Athens knows it's like navigating around the Hampton Court maze, boxed in by lunatics in juggernauts and bumper-cars all shouting and trying to kill you. I soon got used to this, being comforted by the iron girder protection front and back on the Land Rover. I was so busy concentrating on the Greek language, which is not easy when most of the words required will not be found in any dictionary, that I got lost; ten minutes to go. After investigating most of the back streets of Piraeus, some more than once, I found myself spat out on the quay side; five minutes to go. This, however, is nothing like the quay in Amorgos, where with a run, a skip and a jump you're in the water.

Being at the quay in Piraeus is like being at the entrance tunnel to Heathrow and having to find your own aircraft on the tarmac without any signs or assistance. Fortunately having spent many happy hours/days/months waiting for ships in Piraeus, I had a fair idea where I should be but it was a classic case of not being in a good position to start off from.

I battled through the affray and eventually saw my ship on the horizon; three minutes to go. Approaching the berth I realised with horror that I'd passed the turning and was facing three lines of traffic coming off the quay going into the city on a one way system which was not the way I favoured; two minutes to go and so close. With the prospect of two more days on the quay, I took a sharp turn towards the city, slammed the vehicle into reverse and backed into the mass of traffic heading off the quay. OK I was progressing, as the police like to put it, in the wrong direction, but at least I was pointing the right way. With only wing mirrors being effective I couldn't see what was happening directly behind me, but it was certainly very interesting to see the devastation on the pavements on either side as I went past. Amazingly nothing was damaged. The other drivers saw it was a British Land Rover, complete with the union flag on either side, but I think they were so taken aback by the manoeuvre that they assumed I had to be Athenian and just carried on swearing as usual. Now I was 100 metres from the ship's ramp but with no ticket; one minute to go. I jumped out and ran to the ticket office. I passed a few port policemen who seemed interested in chatting to me about something, but I had no time for engaging in pleasantries with these generally very helpful gentlemen. The ticket office was full. Adopting my new found Athenian habits, I threw everyone aside and demanded a ticket; 30 seconds to go, it was going to be tight. The agent said he couldn't sell me a ticket. Practicing a little more of my un-publishable Greek, I explained that I was going to get that ferry even if I had to kill him; 15 seconds to go. He was quite calm actually, I guess in that job he'd been threatened with worse in the past. He said I couldn't have a ticket because we were storm bound and the ship would not leave until the morning. I thanked him, wandered out and ordered a beer at the taverna next door; 12 hours to go! The police seemed to have forgotten about why they wanted a chat, which was a shame really, as they could have bought the beer.

After a very uncomfortable, but quiet, night in the Land Rover, I was awoken by the usual sounds and noises of a busy and active Piraeus. Clearly it was all action stations again. I went into the ticket office, fortunately finding a new clerk and requested a ticket for Naxos, the closest I could get to Amorgos that day. He picked up a pre-printed ticket for a car and one person, crossed out the name of the ship and the time of departure and added the correct details. No further information was asked for and I left the office with a ticket for Mr Popodopulas and his Robin Reliant. I climbed into the three wheeled Land Rover, tried to look Greek and headed for the ramp. By this time it was bedlam. This was the first ship to head for the Cyclades in three days and everyone wanted to get on it. Cars were pushing forward and vying for the few places still available from the previous day's loading. The port police were blowing their whistles, the ship's officers were shouting for calm and trying to sort out priorities, it was only a matter of time before someone or something ended up in the water. Many of the cars and lorries had arrived that morning and in a lull I explained that I had been waiting all night by the ramp. I was told to park at the side, whereupon about six cars forced themselves in front of me, that's what happens when you drive a Robin Reliant instead of a long-wheel base Land Rover. I remained calm and very British, but stood next to the ramp officer reminding him of my existence. My patience paid off and I got one of the six places available, I realised later why they favoured my vehicle when I found cargo piled high on the flat bonnet. There were bundles of newspapers, boxes of fruit and perched right on the top of it all was someone's large suitcase. I was now in the comfortable situation of being able to go on board and watch what to me now was the entertainment unveiling itself on the ramp from the deck above. Places were allocated, vehicles being carefully selected to ensure maximum capacity, much to the annoyance of the more wealthy passengers with Mercedes and large BMWs. One chap tried three times to push his motorbike onto the ship and was told there was no room. His wife started diversionary tactics by chatting up the deck officer whilst he snuck behind him with the bike. He was spotted by another deck hand. He and his bike were literally thrown off the ship. His wife was still on the ramp as it was going up. She shouted to the officer that her husband was not on board so she got thrown off as well. We were on our way.

At the end of 2000 we went back to the UK again for the winter. This time we decided to leave the Land Rover on Amorgos – never again across Europe at a deafening 65 kilometres per hour. I was more used to driving from Athens to the UK enjoying the comfort of a flight deck in three and a half hours, not three and a half days. We decided to take Henri's Peugeot from the UK for the next year's journey, as it would be a more practical vehicle for running around on Amorgos when we didn't have clients. This time it was ship to Piraeus, train to Patras, ship to Ancona and hire car to Calais, train across the channel and drive to Oxford. Sounded easy, but of course we didn't put in the Delahunt-Rimmer fudge factor. We had the same procedure for packing up the house and the now familiar farewells. This time however, it seemed to be Amber that most people were sad to see leave. She had become very adept at chasing stray cats out of tavernas, but never touching them. We had to spend the first night in Athens. I had tasked our agents there to find us a hotel that would take dogs. This is not easy in Athens and clearly came under the 'too difficult' bracket, as when we arrived at the hotel the staff had no knowledge of a dog.

Whilst Amber lay on the pristine shiny marble floor at reception in this five star hotel, the manager was called. He was absolutely charming, but adamant that dogs were not allowed in the hotel. Then as Amber lay there, trying to look as cute as possible without a single snarl, the manager softened. As it happened, earlier that year there had been a very bad earthquake in Greece and British Welsh Border Collies had been brought in as rescue dogs to search for survivors under the rubble in Athens. I have no idea how the manager got the impression that Amber was one of these dogs returning home having stayed on to train the local dogs, but he did. The owner was called, and under the exceptional circumstances, he said that he would consider it an honour if this very brave dog would stay at his hotel for the night.

We had planned on the high-speed train from Piraeus to Patras, which takes just one hour. Wrong, the high-speed doesn't have a guard's van and the van is the only place in which dogs are allowed to travel on a train. We had to take the slow train, which took four hours, stopping at every station en route. We tried to sneak Amber into a carriage at the last minute, but the guard spotted us as he was blowing the whistle. All three of us were unceremoniously bungled into the guard's van. This was about a metre off the ground. I gave Henri a leg up, launched her into the air and she landed in a heap on the floor of the van. The considerable amount of baggage got the same treatment, the only difference was that they didn't grunt on impact and complain. This left myself and Amber on the platform as the train started to move. Amber followed the same trajectory as Henri and the baggage and she didn't seem to mind. Then I had to run to keep up with the departing train and haul myself through the open sliding doorway. In the cowboy movies you always get to do this from a horse, but there wasn't even a donkey in sight to assist. We spent four hours in an open guard's van sitting on folding down seats. At one point we ran over something. The train came to a screeching halt. Men ran up and down the train and were peering under it from our open doors. Shoulders were shrugged, hands were cast upwards in a gesture of, 'don't know', or 'what can we do anyway?' and we continued our merry little, very slow, way. We never found out what we had run over, but there were some terrible graunching sounds as we pulled away. Amber crossed the Adriatic under the bed in our cabin again. We hired a car in Ancona and drove across Europe in relative comfort stopping in Calais for Amber's veterinary check, which was required 24 hours before entering the UK. We took the left hand drive car on the train to Dover, where we swapped it for a British vehicle and drove on to Oxford.

The winter of 2000/2001 was spent in the UK and in February 2001 we packed Henri's Peugeot to the gunnels for the now familiar drive across Europe. After locking up the house well before dawn, I leapt into the driver's seat and shouted, 'all aboard for the Oxford to Amorgos Express'. Henri leapt in, but Amber didn't. She sat on the drive with her head on one side, as if to say, 'and where do I sit?' We had forgotten to leave a space for her. She travelled all the way across Europe and the Peloponnese in the passenger foot well. She was actually so comfortable there she started to prefer it from then on, even when the car was empty.

In November of 2001, we drove Henri's Peugeot back to the UK for our last winter there. Uneventful? Of course not. A few kilometres from Calais, in fog, a stag jumped over the central reservation straight into our path. Henri was driving and at the time I was looking at the map with my head down. There was nothing she could have done. The car was written off, unfortunately the stag wasn't, he limped away. A motorway maintenance vehicle passing the other way stopped, and as the road was very quiet, he came across to us. He called the police who arrived very quickly. They couldn't have been more helpful. Henri said, 'I just didn't see it and I was driving very slowly'. The senior of the two said in good English, 'Are you both OK?' 'Fine', we said. Amber was of course in the passenger foot well and in the circumstances probably the safest place. 'You were very lucky', he said. 'One second earlier and he would have been straight through the windscreen and you would both have been killed. I have seen it too many times on this stretch of road'. We looked at each other, Amber just looked for the stag to chase. 'Are you sure that you are OK?' he said.

To us it was just a crump, the fact that it had been a close call was irrelevant to us. We had both been in close calls in the military, myself quite a few times. The junior officer got a shot gun out of their car boot to try to locate and destroy the injured animal, but unfortunately failed to find it. They were obviously well equipped in this area for this eventuality. As Henri was the driver and owner of the wreck, she was invited into the cop car to 'answer questions'. The policeman couldn't have been more charming. He even asked Henri what type of background music she would prefer on their CD player. Paperwork complete, they called a breakdown truck for us and stayed until it arrived just half an hour later. All three of us were taken in the truck's cab to the garage, where he called his cousin who owned a hotel. Accommodation was arranged and we were picked up by the owner and taken there. I phoned the insurance company in the UK and requested clearance to hire a car to continue our journey. They refused to approve this until the car was assessed as a write-off. They wouldn't take the word of a 'Frog' and wanted the car repatriating to the UK. We hired a car anyway and continued our journey to the port.

We planned to go as foot passengers on the ship and pick up a right hand drive car in Dover and drop it off in

Oxford. Wrong – animals had to travel in a car, not on foot. OK, no problem, we would take the left hand drive car to Dover and swap it over there as we had the previous year. Wrong – they already had too many there. 'Illegal immigrants, no doubt' I said to Henri. OK, we would hire a right hand drive car in Calais that someone had brought across and take it back all the way to Oxford. Wrong – none available. The following day Henri got on the Sea France ferry and went to Dover. She then hired a right hand drive car and drove it onto the next Sea France ferry and crossed back to Calais. She was then to pick up me, Amber and the luggage and get on the last Sea France ferry back to Dover. You may think that it wasn't very chivalrous of me to offer to take on this mission myself, but I didn't want to leave a single lady guarding a dog and luggage in the port of Calais. Apart from that, there was this really nice pub there which served good old British beer, and I was more experienced with being behind enemy lines than Henri. The barmaid, Charlene, was a stunning young French girl, tall and slim with long auburn hair. She was exquisitely dressed in a very low-cut blouse and an extremely short skirt. She actually worked for the French resistance and had an escape plan for us should Henri fail to return. Personally, I had no wish to escape, I was quite happy where I was. Henri returned, and took me away. That day she had sailed on all three of the Sea France's fleet, but didn't receive a single medal for it. I did however give her a mention in dispatches, whilst Charlene received the Croix de Guerre for looking after me.

That winter of 2001/2002 was our last winter in the UK. Over the next decade we went back a few times, but only for a couple of weeks at a time for business and to see family and friends. Also briefly once for my mother's funeral and once when my father was taken ill.

Chapter XXXI No more UK

In the winters we huddled up to our wood burning stove, and in the summers enjoyed the balmy evenings on our patio overlooking the bay. One day our favorite taverna had a 'no notice' spot inspection to check on the papers for the staff. Of course, none of them have papers as they are only employed for the very high season and are all paid cash in hand. Fortunately the police chief uses our local taverna, and he warned the owner about the no notice inspection the day before. So at the prescribed time the owner sent all his staff to the beach for an hour. As the chief now knew everything would be in order, he saved some time by just driving past waving.

One morning I had to lug two big gas bottles from the front of the house, where they had been delivered, round to the back. I was dripping in sweat and my back was killing me. I couldn't make too much of a fuss about it, though, as the gentleman who delivered them and whipped them down off his donkey was 89 years old and was wearing a thick shirt and pullover. It is best not to get a chill at that age, I guess. We should have had enough gas for two months, but the fridge gobbles it up in these temperatures. And of course, a gas fridge kicks out a fair amount of heat from the back, which heats up the room even more, so it is kind of working against itself. When I went to change the bottle, I found the connection on it was broken, so the poor donkey who had lugged it all this way had to take it back again. We didn't like to tell it. Due to in-breeding we have a few cerebrally challenged islanders, but they are all donkey handlers and as happy as pigs in the proverbial. The trouble is only their donkeys understand them. The chap who then normally did the donkey runs for us refused to understand that he had to take a full bottle away and so his father came. Unfortunately, the old man thought that this bottle was dangerous and it took a lot of persuasion to get him to load it. The donkey wasn't very happy either and ran away with two empty bottles aboard trailing ropes behind him. Eventually we got it sorted and we just hoped there wasn't going to be a mushroom cloud coming up from the gorge as he went around the corner.

The year 2001 was unusual as Greek Orthodox Easter fell on the same date as the Catholic Easter, 15th April. The two movable holidays can be as many as five weeks apart. The festival starts on Good Friday, with the bier being paraded around the villages, but the real fun starts at midnight on Saturday, after the services end. Everyone comes out of church, the doors are closed and the priest calls for the evil spirits to come out. Someone is left inside who is then supposed to throw open the doors, signifying the spirits leaving the church. Two years previous, they had played a trick on the priest and the chap inside refused to open the doors. The more the crowd laughed, the more angry the priest became, he was not a happy priest that year. A candle is then lit from the church, and everyone passes the sacred flame on by lighting each other's candles, the congregation then parade around the village by candlelight and mark a sooty cross on the doorway of each house. Firecrackers are thrown, and one year they were even throwing sticks of dynamite. Actually, it all gets a bit dangerous. Everyone then goes home for the Easter dinner of stuffed kid (goat not child).

Vangelis, our friend who owns Celini, had been campaigning for years to have the road in front of his establishment closed to traffic, as parked cars blocked his diner's view of the sea. The mayor had a row of flower tubs put along the end of the road to achieve this . When Vangelis came to work on his motorbike (a commute of at least 100 metres), he turned the corner and went straight over the tubs, landing in a heap in front of his establishment. He then complained to the mayor for not telling him, thus causing his undignified arrival. He pushed home his complaint about the development, by complaining that people could not now drive to his restaurant which would limit his trade. Who would want to be a mayor here?

Amber took to life on Amorgos instantly. As a Border Collie, she was always very energetic. At home in the UK, she would usually get a long walk every morning and go running with us in the fields in the evenings. When we were both working all day, or I was away down the route, she would go to work with Henri. At weekends when it was quiet, she would lie under the console in the air traffic control tower at Northolt. Her occasional bark was sometimes accidentally transmitted and it was not unknown for pilots to send her greetings. During the week, when it was busier, she would stay with the RAF police dogs in the compound next to ATC. This was a problem. She watched them training and thought it was standard procedure to jump up and grab you by the arm, even if you weren't wearing a padded suit. Fortunately, when she moved to Amorgos we managed to get her out of that habit, but not before a few incidents. She did not forget her initial sheepdog training, though. She always went walking with us and our clients in the mountains and obviously loved it. Knowing all our standard walks, she would lead the way, rendering our presence as guides pretty well superfluous. We could have said, 'just follow Amber' and waited in a taverna for their return. If it was hot, she would rush on ahead and lie in the shade, waiting for us to catch up. She was much better than us at keeping people moving. If anyone was trailing behind, she would rush to the back and snap at their heels. That got them to shift. Now if we had done this, there would have been complaints, but

Amber seemed to get away with it. The goatherds are very concerned about dogs in the mountains worrying their animals, but they all knew Amber. They knew that she was a trained sheep dog and no threat. Our clients were very worried about the goatherd's big dogs, but they also knew Amber. Most of the shepherds' dogs are male, and she would behave like a real tart with them, which meant that they forgot all about their aggressive nature and indeed our clients. She would move goats off the path in a controlled manner to clear the way for our clients, but never chase them.

Now cats were a different matter. In tavernas Amber was employed to stop the stray cats from begging at tables. There are hundreds. She was only allowed to operate under strict supervision. Lying by our side, she would watch the cats gathering around the tables, and would be shaking in anticipation like a jelly. On the command 'go, go, go!' she would accelerate from nought to a hundred faster than a Ferrari and scatter the cats to all corners of the island, but would never pursue them beyond the perimeter of the taverna. She would then return and circle all the tables to ensure that there were none hiding, and then return to our side. We had to be careful that there were no children playing with the cats when executing this operation as they would have suffered the same fate and some parents may not have wanted to go and retrieve their little darlings from up a tree. To this end, there was a strict understanding that only Henri, I and the taverna owners were allowed to activate this cruise missile. She never actually touched the cats, but she did get a bloody nose on a few occasions from their very sharp claws. Lizards were far less dangerous. At rest stops on walks, Amber would hunt and then chase them from bush to bush. They liked to dive under the protective Greek spiny spurge, which is very low dense and spiky. When this happened Amber would gently put a front paw onto the bush and shake it until the lizard shot out, and then the game would continue.

It wasn't all fun and games, though. Nikos decided to buy some fertilised turkey eggs and hatch them in an incubator on his farm. When the twelve orphans made an appearance, his elderly mother was nominated as guardian. Amber took pity on her trying to gather together all these unruly children and, unprompted, went to her assistance and had them rounded up in no time. Everyone loved Amber and Amber loved everyone, except cats and fat people; we never worked out why the latter. At least it gave them some well needed exercise being chased up trees!

As mentioned, all our groups seem to get on extremely well together. Also they all seem to develop some sort of theme or interest together. There had been the 'Andrex Points' group, the 'Singing' group, the 'Donkey Saddle Inspection' group and then we had the 'Limerick' group which resulted in the following:

In Amorgos the natives are kind,
The tavernas are easy to find,
The donkeys are cute
But they don't give a hoot
About toilets - look out! Never mind.

There was a young lady from Minoa
Reputed to be quite a goer
She had this red light
Which she lit up at night
And shepherds for miles got to know her.

Amber, the princess of dogs,
Likes sniffing and carrying logs
She huffs and she puffs
Drinks out of troughs
And chases Amorgos's mogs

If you've nothing to do,
Then stop at Frou Frou.
Eyes open wide,
at the ice cream supplied,
and Andrea's miniskirt, too.

Chapter XXXII Buying a Ruin

The ruin next to our house in Stroumbos had been up for sale for decades. In fact, Sonia and Ferruccio had looked at it as a possible renovation before they settled on our house. The threat of a renovation so close to our house would cause us a year of disruption and noise. We had been in Stroumbos two years now, and we had experienced this once before. A very difficult French woman renovated in front of us. She didn't manage the project. She was not even here to put up with the pandemonium. Our very precious water was stolen for the work. Building materials were piled right in front of our door, rubble was dumped on the monopati (path). She has yet to this day to apologise and indeed, apart from the many awful things that this tourist has done to us, she poured a bucket full of dog droppings on our doorstep after we complained to the authorities about her. We can do without tourists like her. Renovation in the village is very expensive. All materials have to be brought in by donkey, at ten euros per donkey per trip. This, of course, takes some time and more than doubles the price of the materials. Additionally, water has to be found, or donkeyed in, or 'stolen'! When our house was built, Sonia and Ferruccio, at the end of a hard working day, made multiple trips to the spring and carried the water for the following day.

We were confident that no one would want to buy the ruin. A few people came to look at it, and when we explained the difficulties, they backed down. Then came a huffing and puffing fat American couple. She was very pleasant and said 'where is the road?' 'We haven't got one', I said. Henri commented 'You have to walk here the same way you have just come'.

That was the end of the matter, we thought, she was already walking away. But not him. 'Gee, it would be real cool to have a holiday home here'. All right, I thought, let's start the speech.

'Look it is very difficult, you need water, you need donkeys, you need permission, and you need so many things it will cost a bomb'. 'Money is not a problem' he retorted. And so they left. And so we put in an offer. Carolina, our only full time neighbour in Stroumbos, was acting as the agent for the vendor. The lady's family used to live here, but she now lives on the island of Iraklia, which is nearby but three hours by ship. The asking price was actually very reasonable, but we made the mistake of haggling. Once these people get set on a sum of money, they will not shift. This delightful lady, Kiria Anna, and her charming husband Dimitris, were quite elderly and wanted the money for their family. We had the money in the building society, so obtaining it was not a problem. We argued over a very small percentage through the long suffering Carolina for a year. In the end, Carolina said, 'Look just buy it at the asking price and I will knock off my commission'. She didn't want more development in Stroumbos, either. Given this kind offer and the interest gained on our money in the bank, we would effectively be paying the offered price. Face was saved on both sides and we made the offer in the autumn of 2001.

Now for the problem of the purchase. They wanted to do this in Naxos. We would have to go there to pay the tax anyway, so this was no problem. We got on the ship for the five hour journey and called in at Iraklia. There were only a few people on the quay. At the front of the queue was a little old couple who were wearing pairs of the largest matching sunglasses you have ever seen. There could be no doubt that it was them. Once they had boarded, I went and introduced myself. Carolina's description was exactly right, the lady was enchanting the gentleman was a little gruff, but no problem, this was a business deal. All the paperwork was prepared at the notary's office in Naxos. It required some coordination as we had to have a lawyer each, we had to have an interpreter, there was the notary of course and the four of us. Eight people in all eventually crammed onto seats in the office. Amber slept under the desk. It had been quite an operation to get there, and even more so to get all these people together at the same time. Everyone held their breath, as the notary went through the papers. She looked up at us, then looked across at the old couple and back to us. 'There's a problem' she said. 'OK' I said 'I'm sure it can be resolved'. 'It is just that they do not own the property it has already been sold' she said in English. They had owned another property in Stroumbos, which had been sold to a German gentleman. By mistake this ruin, some distance away, had been included in the deal. It was just before Christmas, and we think they were planning on giving this little windfall to their children and grandchildren. The difficulty was explained to them in Greek. Poor Anna burst into tears, little old Dimitris jumped up with great agility for his age and started banging his fist on the table, saying it wasn't true. He woke up Amber, who started barking.

'OK, OK,' said the notary, 'let's think about this. These are very honest people and I can see there has been a mistake. You may if you wish go ahead with the purchase anyway'. They were friends of Carolina and I could see that there had been a mistake. Also we were friends of the German lady who now owned her late brother's house. We knew that she would not lay claim to the ruin in question. 'However', I said, 'if we subsequently sell, our ownership could be in question '. The notary and lawyers agreed. 'There is another way' she said. 'They can give it to their son and then he can sell it to you'. 'Great' I said, with relief, looking at my watch not wanting to miss the ship. 'How long will it take you to draft out the papers?' The notary said, 'not long, but you will have to wait ten years before he can sell it to you'. More tears, more desk bashing. 'There is yet another way' she said. 'It can be resolved through a magistrate, but it will take a few months'. I said that I would put down a deposit. The notary, a government official, said 'that's not a good idea, because then you will have to declare to me exactly what you are paying for purchase tax purposes'. I turned to the couple and said, 'please will you hold it for us and we promise we will buy it in the spring'. Kiria Anna, whom we had only met two hours previous, hugged and kissed us. Dimitris extracted his fist from the inkwell and shook my hand. Smiles all round, and the eight of us agreed to start again a few months later.

In the spring of 2002, after our final winter in the UK, we tried again. This time we didn't notice them on the quay as we went through Iraklia, even though we were on the deck because of Amber. Just as we were pulling out of the port on the way to Naxos, a lady came up to us and said, 'are you buying a ruin in Stroumbos on Amorgos?' 'Yes' we said. It was Kiria Anna's daughter. She was going to make sure everything was OK this time around, and she had been sent to find an English looking couple with a red Welsh Border Collie, this was not a difficult mission on a nearly empty ship. The couple wanted to ensure that we were on board. I went down to see them, hugs and kisses and hand shaking again. On arrival in Naxos we went to the bank and filled the briefcase with money. Then onto the notary's office, where the group of eight assembled again! This time, Amber avoided the desk. The problem had been resolved, it was just the formalities to be completed. I had to proffer my passport and tax papers. Kiria Anna had to proffer her proof of identity and tax papers. 'What tax papers?' she said. 'Well I need your tax number' said the notary. 'I am retired and don't pay tax'. 'To sell a building you have to have a tax number' said the notary. Dimitris started to leap up again,

Amber shot into the outer office in anticipation of the forthcoming outburst. We thought, 'yet another wasted journey'. 'Wait' said the notary in an authoritative voice. 'It is not a problem; all you have to do is go to the tax office here in Naxos and register. It will only take you an hour'. I have never seen two little old people move so fast. In fact, to be honest, I didn't see them move. I think I must have blinked, because one second they were there and when I opened my eyes again, they were not.

One hour or so later, the congregation was again assembled. Papers were completed and signed, as we had done for our first house. The vendor signed every sheet of paper, so did I, so did the two lawyers, the interpreter and the notary. The deal was done. We had all signed for a said amount of money to be handed over. We had signed that if it was more, we would be subject to a fine or even imprisonment.

'How much are they actually paying you?' whispered Kyria Anna's lawyer to her. She told him and the briefcase was opened. Her lawyer counted out the wads of money, one by one in front of the other lawyer and the notary - the government official! It was clear to all that it was more than declared. As the first wad was counted, it was placed on the desk. Dimitris took off his hat and slammed it on top, presumably to avoid any sleight of hand by the lawyer. This procedure was repeated for every wad. When the count was complete, a shopping bag was produced and the pile of notes was swept from under the hat into it and it was very quickly zipped up in case there was any other funny business. Handshakes and kisses all around and an offer of lunch for us by Kyria Anna. It was a pleasure to hand money over to such a nice old couple.

One year later, at eight o'clock in the morning, we got a telephone call from our neighbor Carolina. She said, 'you've got some friends on their way to see you'. We opened the door and there was Kyria Anna and Kyrios Dimitris. They were visiting the island and had walked all the way to Stroumbos just to see us.

The Iris centre above Celini offers, amongst other things; yoga, massage and meditation. It also hosts 'wacky' groups. That summer of 2002 one such Swedish group was spending 30 minutes each morning screaming as loud as they could, and then they were not allowed to speak for the rest of the day. For the record, these groups have now been banned from most establishments, because of the noise so early in the morning, which is detrimental to guests' hangovers. This also presents some problems when ordering meals, particularly when something is not on the menu and can't be pointed to. This was causing Vangelis at Celini and his staff significant problems, and considerably slowing down the service. It had also resulted in a number of errors. How the lady who wanted toast and marmalade at breakfast got an omelette, we are still trying to fathom out. It had also stretched Vangelis' patience, which had frequently resulted in frayed tempers. A British couple ordered spaghetti bolognaise, this incidentally was a verbally transmitted request. Peter the East German, a very slow and deep voiced waiter passed the request to the kitchen. 'We're out of it' shouted Vangelis, 'give them chips'. Peter sauntered over with a plate of chips slammed it on the table and said in a very slow deep voice, 'no spaghetti' and walked off. The couple were so taken aback, they just ate them unquestioningly. One wonders how Michael Winner would have dealt with this approach. On the fourth morning, there was no screaming, the group came to breakfast announcing that they had now passed onto another stage and they could now talk. Breakfast was ordered in the normal fashion, but Vangelis decided to retaliate and played the true dumb waiter. An hour later, the screaming started again.

Everyone was taken aback as after the breakfast announcement, we had assumed that the rest of the village could now get some peace and quiet, until we realised that it was a couple having a domestic, no doubt they didn't talk after this either. Unfortunately, Vangelis didn't realise this, and thought that they had another wacky group. Later that day, he had a customer who was giving all the sign language again. Retaliating again he also pretended to be dumb. Unfortunately this customer was genuinely deaf and dumb – oops.

Ivana, our Polish friend, had some money transferred from the USA to the only bank here. It somehow went to the wrong bank, and the banks don't trust each other. For example, we once had a bankers draft from an Irish client drawn on the Commercial Bank of Greece. Our bank, the Agricultural Bank, would not recognise it, and wanted us to pay to have it sent to Athens and the money transferred from the Commercial Bank of Greece to them. Also, they were confused about where this place 'Ireland' was. Only by telling them that it was in England would they even take it. Ivana said that she needed the money urgently, not in two weeks time. After about two packets of cigarettes and much muttering, the cashier went to a cupboard behind her and pulled out a carrier bag stuffed with bits of paper and piles of dosh. She scribbled on a piece of paper chucked it in the bag and pulled out the required amount of cash and handed it over. A trainee cashier asked what this procedure was, which she obviously hadn't been taught at college in Athens, and it was explained that this was the 'can't deal with it now file'.

Some years later, we went into the bank to get cash to pay for some building work. Costas, the chief cashier, said, 'I'm sorry, you can't draw that amount'. It was 1,000 euros, but we had plenty in our account to cover it. Henri said, 'why not, what is the problem? Are we limited to how much we can draw each day?' 'No', said Costas, 'that is not the problem, it is just that we only have 400 euros and we may need that for tourists'. 'I thought you were a bank', said Henri, 'you are supposed to have that stuff called money'. 'Well we haven't' said Costas, 'your builder won't mind waiting for the money and you can just run up tabs at shops and tavernas'. So we left without any money. Costas was quite right, of course, many people run up bills, and it had taken us over a month to get the bill off our builder, which even then was scribbled on a scrap of paper.

We went to Katapola and ended up with packages for nine other people, including 10 tons of peanuts for Carolina, our neighbour in Stroumbos, for the festival of Agios Nikitas, which she hosts every year. We had some paint for Mario, a German artist, but he only wanted the cheapest. It was so cheap that it didn't work, and then it was our entire fault that the greatest artist in the world had come to a grinding halt in his finest hour! Len, the painter and decorator, said that the cheapest paint he would ever put on even a German's wall was twice the price. We also got a box of glasses for Vangelis. He wanted 30 and the standard box is 48, so Lefteris, in the hardware shop, took out 18, resealed it, dropped it, opened it, then took out 18 broken ones, put in the ones originally taken out, resealed it and I managed to get it to the car in one piece before he got a chance to get anywhere near it again. Lefteris may have an economics degree from a top university in the UK but he is not a very good juggler!

The big snappy news; I was at Nikos' taverna asking Michael-Anne, the hotel office manager, if he was there and she said he was out fishing. I asked if he ever caught anything, and as usual she was a little derogatory. Michael-Anne is very keen on fly fishing back home in Oregon. She considers that, quote; 'dragging a big hook through the water with a lump of meat on it', is not fishing. Literally 10 minutes later Nikos phoned up on his mobile from Metallio, on the other side of the island, saying that he was towing in a 200 kilogram shark. There was concern that he might lose it, but four hours later, he came into port with a grin from ear to ear. He had caught a 175 kilogram one the previous year; this had been weighed. He didn't want this one weighing though, probably because when landed, he could see that it was slightly smaller than last year, the consensus of opinion was that it was about 150 kilograms, though it was very impressive. It was killed and butchered in a very Greek fashion with bits of flesh flying everywhere and everyone wielding knives and choppers all at once, and certainly not in unison, or in harmony, come to that. We went for dinner, of course. Nikos grilled the tail steaks outside over charcoal, Mario insisted on being fed as soon as possible and so got a small one from the end, and complained like mad when we got a huge one an hour later. The following day, he asked how much we paid and was even more annoyed when we told him that Nikos would not accept payment from us. It was in fact, in return for the photographs of 'the catch', but we didn't reveal this business deal to Mario.

We had a medical evacuation to deal with, the result of which was very reassuring. A Dutch friend of ours who came here twice a year was taken very ill. Len called his drinking mate the quack, who diagnosed pneumonia and prescribed vitamins and bed rest! He was staying in the gardens on the beach, so we had him moved next to Swedish Christina, where she could keep an eye on him. Len accused us of going against this great doctor's orders by moving him, and asked us what did we think we were doing interfering. Three days later, Christina was very concerned about the patient and asked Henri to look in on him. Henri diagnosed the first stages of heart failure and many other complications. We got Vangelis to phone the doctor to get a note for his insurance company. The doctor said, 'I am on siesta', and slammed the phone down. Henri spoke to 'proper' doctors in Amsterdam, Athens and Santorini and they agreed with her diagnosis. It was getting too late in the evening for a helicopter, so the insurance company said they would send a fast boat. We were expecting a coast guard vessel or something military. We were waiting for it on the quay at midnight, and this Crown 'gin palace' thing comes zooming in, very, very impressive. Also two doctors with all the emergency equipment. The lady doctor was also very, very impressive! She was a stunning blonde, wearing a short white doctor's coat, suspenders and stockings. OK, maybe I imagined the latter, however I suddenly decided that I didn't feel very well either, but nobody took any notice of me. So that was the way that we got him away; by medevac 'gin palace' to Santorini, where they were going to stabilise him in hospital, and then by an aircraft waiting there to take him to Athens. He was in Athens for three weeks until he was fit enough to move to a hospital in Holland. When I told Nikos at the taverna about the lady doctor on the boat, he said that he didn't feel very well either. Henri said that we were a bunch of tarts. Throughout the whole operation, Len accused us of interfering and why didn't we call the doctor again. He said that Henri didn't know what she was talking about and didn't speak to us again for weeks. And it was all because we made his drinking mate, the doctor, look the idiot he was. When we told Len a few weeks later about the patient still being too ill to move from Athens, he started to reflect on the matter. Henri had a telephone call from the gentleman's son a month later to thank her. It appears that her actions had saved his life. He visited Amorgos again the following year, but he was still very sick. We never heard from him, or saw him again, after that.

Chapter XXXIII Weather

The weather on Amorgos is unique in the Cyclades due to the geomorphological features of the island. Its orientation dictates that air masses reaching the area are affected differently than they are on other nearby islands. It is the driest of all the islands, receiving approximately only 340 millimetres of rainfall a year. This doesn't mean that Amorgos is barren however, indeed quite the opposite. The geological structure maintains the winter rains, resulting in a green and fertile island covered in flowers in the spring. The east/west orientation of the 800 metre high mountain ridge results in moisture forming by orographic lifting in the prevailing northerly meltemi summer winds. Consequently, the autumn bulbs flower in the late summer even before the first rains have arrived. Greece is not, however, 'summer all year around', as some tour operators would wish you to believe. On Amorgos it is not unknown to be able to lie in the sun on the beach on Christmas day. However, it is also not unknown for there to be a covering of snow on said beach in February. Nevertheless, we do undeniably enjoy a long dry summer with many hours of sunshine.

It was the eve of Valentine's Day 2004. After a full day in the office, we were enjoying a sundowners beer. The sky was black and so was the mood in Celini. Vangelis had just returned from Athens where he had, at great expense, purchased a new pair of spectacles. He was complaining that he couldn't see a single thing through them. Suggestions were made that perhaps the optician had given him the wrong prescription. Suggestions were made that perhaps he had picked up someone else's glasses by mistake. No suggestions were made about his sobriety, as he is virtually teetotal. Only days later did he discover the protective removable film on the lenses. We observed a white substance descending from the sky. Vangelis did not of course. Being British, we knew only too well what it was, but on Amorgos? Snow is virtually unknown here. At the most it happens every ten years. We thought perhaps it was a freak flurry, but no, it continued for hours. The beach was completely white and it was getting quite deep on the roads up to the mountain villages. Children under ten had to be trained in the ancient art of snowman making, but no training was required in snowball fights, which caught on very fast. In order to avoid the inevitable missiles and to drive back up to Langada without getting stuck, we disappeared fast. The sunset was very dramatic. The sky started to clear and the setting red sun was reflected off the snow.

The following morning there were clear blue skies and everything was white. I had woken up early and the temptation to get into the snow-covered mountains was irresistible. Henri had a cold and it took a lot of persuasion to get her out of bed to experience this opportunity. We went, and she didn't die. She did insist on delaying our departure to make a flask of soup though. We walked up to the monastery of Theologos. The views were spectacular. The ancient wine press there had icicles hanging from it. We walked up higher and looked down on the snow covered island. The snow was only five centimetres deep up there and in fact made walking very easy as the stony path was smooth. It was melting very fast but still bitterly cold. In the villages the melting snow had turned into ice and proved treacherous to pedestrians and donkeys alike. The hotel owner's elderly father, Manolis, was concerned about his goats up in the mountains. He set off on his donkey, which promptly did the splits. He got off and slid all over the place himself. He ended up using the donkey as a Zimmer frame with each supporting the other. As he descended out of the village he decided that it was all too dangerous, the goats could fend for themselves, and turned back. This was not an option; every one step forward donkey and man slid back two. The goats won the day.

By lunchtime we were sitting outside a taverna in blazing sunshine in shirt sleeves. Children were showing us icicles that were now beginning to melt and were having great fun in smashing them on the ground. They will probably be twenty the next time they experience this phenomenon.

When we collected the 'snow' photographs from Katapola everyone was amazed. 'You went into the mountains in the snow?', 'Trelos!' ('Crazy!'). In the Royal Air Force I have dug and slept in snow holes in white out conditions. Walking in five centimetres of snow with clear blue skies is Girl Guide material. Theologos is Papa Spirithon's favourite spot on the island, as indeed it is ours. We were having a coffee, OK a beer, in Katapola and looking at the photos and I said to Henri 'Papa Spirithon would love to see these. I bet he has never been there in the snow'. 'What is the best way to get some copies to him?' At that moment he drove past in his battered monastery van. It must at this point go on record that he is the worst driver on the island and this takes some doing. Even the policemen have been known to roll their cars. To our knowledge the priest however has never had an accident, but we presume someone is looking after him. I found him in the hardware shop and presented him with one of the pictures. He was delighted but said 'you went up to Theologos in the snow? Trelos!' He asked if there were any more photos. The photography shop had wanted to keep the negatives to make copies for themselves, and I informed him of this. Henri went back to the shop to order some extra copies for our friends and found him there ordering a full set. It was a good job it wasn't summer with a shot of Henri topless on the beach. He said 'did you go up there as well in the snow?' 'Yes of course' she said. The word 'trelos' was used again. We kept asking for the negatives back, but more and more people heard of their existence. I think it took two months before they were eventually returned to us.

We do not have a meteorological observation station on Amorgos, but on Thursday night 22nd January 2004, Naxos reported winds of 185 kilometres per hour and with our meteorological training, we would assess it was about the same here. The wind was however only a minor problem and there was very little damage in the mountain villages at our end of the island. The biggest problem was the sea state of Beaufort 12.

The damage in the port of Ormos Aegialis was substantial. The local opinion was pretty unanimous that it had not been so bad for more than 100 years. The problem was a combination of the sea state and the swell direction (from the northwest) which was directed straight into the bay and at the harbour.

The first third of the harbour wall along the quay was destroyed. It was a substantial wall, constructed of piles of very large boulders the size of a small car. The boulders were smashed onto the quay by the mountainous and forceful waves. One boulder was shot straight across the quay and landed on a fishing boat, which of course sank. One other boat sank, another ashore was destroyed and many other boats were damaged, even the ones they managed to get out of the water in time. One was blown across the road taking a lamp post with it. The quay was strewn with rocks and boulders, damaged fishing nets and rubbish. The quay had lumps missing, cracks and at least three football sized holes. The beach was of course strewn with broken bits of boats and rubbish.

Only one establishment in the village was flooded. Tavernas on the beach sustained a little damage and one was particularly bad. We spoke to the owner, Mimis, who is never fazed, and true to form, the following day he was smiling and getting on with the rebuilding. All the benches in the port and along the front had gone. It looked like a war zone. It was, however, quite amazing how fast the authorities moved to put things right. One week later everything was back to normal.

These storms cause many power cuts, but this doesn't of course affect us in Stroumbos. One day we went to the old shop in Tholaria and their electric scales were out. They were using the old fashioned hand held scales where you hang a weight on one end, the produce on the other and move the balance weight up and down the arm. They had lost the set of weights, and so weighed our tomatoes using a kilo packet of spaghetti as the weight.

In 2009 we were commissioned to write a guidebook to Amorgos. This was published in 2010 under the title, 'Amorgos, The Secret Jewel of the Cyclades: A Visitor's and Walker's Guide.' Later that year I received an e-mail from our financial advisor in the UK, Mike Earnshaw, to say that a famous English historian and broadcaster called Michael Wood had been interviewed on the radio and was asked to name his three favourite Greek islands. He replied, 'Amorgos, Amorgos and Amorgos'. Mike thought that we would like to hear about this interest in our island from a television personality. Having been to Amorgos to see us a few times our advisor knew that we live like peasants with no electricity and, to this end no television, and so asked if we knew of this gentleman or indeed had met him here. We get the occasional glimpse of television in tavernas and the nature and history satellite channels are very popular with the islanders. I thought that I recognised the name of the historian, but assured our advisor that we didn't know him. Then it occurred to me that it would be nice if I sent a copy of our new book to this Michael Wood as an appreciation of the mention of Amorgos on the British radio. I eventually found an e-mail address for him and sent a short letter: 'Dear Mr Wood, I hear that you were recently interviewed by the BBC and had indicated that Amorgos was your favourite Greek island. I understand that you are a regular visitor here, but I don't believe that we have ever met. We have just published a visitor's and walker's guide to Amorgos and, if you like, I would be very pleased to send you a copy'. I received a reply along the lines of: Dear Paul, What do you mean we have never met. We were having a beer together just a few weeks ago. Thank you for your kind offer, but we did actually buy a copy of your book'. We will see you again next year'. We had known a delightful couple named Mike and Rebecca, and their family, for years. We kept bumping into them in the mountains, usually on our way home to Stroumbos. But we never knew who he was in 'real life'. To be honest, we still didn't really know, so I found a few clips of his documentaries on the Internet. I must say, he does come across incredibly well on television! He was jolly decent about our ignorance when we met again the following year.

Chapter XXXIV Mrs M

As mentioned before, all of our clients are generally delightful and more than happy with our product. The worst client we have ever had must go on record. I am not mentioning the year for legal reasons. We will call her Mrs M, although, if she reads this, which I sincerely hope she does, she will recognise herself. Those conversant with the more colourful words of the Greek language will appreciate the given name; I will enlighten readers no further. She was a dumpy, grumpy lady in her mid to late sixties, with a permanent scowl on her face. Her companion was an archetypal English gentleman, a tall, slim and cheerful man of about seventy-five. The problems started as soon as we arrived with her at the hotel. I drove slowly, as I always do with clients, down the very short ramp into the car park and as I parked, she called out to me in a croaky voice, 'you drove down too fast and now I feel dizzy'. For days afterwards, she claimed that she was still feeling dizzy. On that morning we took her and her companion on the first walk of the programme. She said, 'I will walk up the ramp and you can pick me up at the top'. Given that this is only a few metres, of course I agreed. We then drove to the mountain village of Tholaria, where we start the first walk. On the drive she said, 'I thought that this was a group holiday'. I pointed out that this is not mentioned in any of our brochures. And indeed there were two of them, and in my Oxford English dictionary 'two' is a group. It turned out that she had not read the specifications for the programme, which explain repeatedly that it is a walking based holiday, and the simple fact was that she was too unfit to walk even a short distance. Indeed, she had problems walking up the steps to her room. She then informed us that she wanted to paint, not walk, and added, 'I need other people with me for inspiration'. Henri then said that she would take the woman's companion for a walk and get on with the first part of our programme. I said, 'I will stay with you, Mrs M, for your inspiration'. At that point, Mrs M decided that she preferred to be alone.

I stayed anyway. We always throw our clients in at the deep end on day one by taking them to Agiris and Maria's taverna in Tholaria, which is called O Horeftis, or The Dancer. It is very traditional and they are a welcoming and wonderful family. The establishment was very basic and hadn't changed in a hundred years. Unfortunately, neither had the 'facilities'. They had a toilet, with no seat of course, because these are rare apart from in the hotels here. They had toilet paper, they had soap, and the loo flushed - what more does one want? Yes it was a tad smelly, because the local men do not often flush it to save water. It had a door, OK it didn't close, but there was no point anyway, because the large window in the door was missing. But at least people could see if it is occupied or not. Of course, Mrs M began whinging at once about the facilities and totally refused to use them, even though I offered to station a Kalashnikov-bearing, big, hairy, female baboon at the entrance.

The following day, more complaints started rolling in, and her companion was asking for separate rooms, but the hotel was full. I did a counseling session with Mrs M whilst Henri and Graham, our archaeologist, took her friend into the mountains. After thirty minutes, she had talked herself into a circle. 'I suffer from vertigo and can't travel on buses'. 'I can't find a bus timetable'. 'I have been to Greece many times and don't need to be told about the history and culture, and also I don't like Greek food'. 'Your brochure says that you cover history and culture, but you haven't mentioned either of those to me'. In the inevitable letter, actually letters, of complaint, that she wrote upon her return to the UK, she alleged, that we didn't cover archaeology, botany, herbs and ornithology. I said to the excellent holiday company that we market through, 'What did she expect us to do when she wouldn't leave her hotel room?' 'Arrange for a fly past of birds in front of her balcony, get Graham to turn back her carpet to see if he could find an obsidian blade and for Henri to plant orchids in her shower tray?' Having failed to persuade me that she had grounds for complaints, she phoned the holiday company. Poor Steve there got the same diatribe. Again there was nothing he could do apart from phone me. I explained the problem with this semi invalid on a walking based holiday in the mountains of Amorgos.

Having got nowhere with the powers that be, Mrs M started complaining loudly in the hotel restaurant to her long suffering friend about everything. Many of their fellow diners commented about it to the owner. Our friend Mario the artist, sitting five tables away one evening, could clearly hear her carrying on. The hotel manager, Michael-Anne, makes some of the greatest soups in the world but, oh no, Mrs M can make them better. 'They didn't give me bacon with my breakfast,' she said. (She didn't ask.) 'They didn't give us two plates to share a dish.' (She didn't ask.) 'I'm going to put rat poison in her marmalade,' Michael-Anne said. (She didn't.) The hotel owner, Nikos, said that he would never have her back again.(He didn't!) She continued complaining in public about Henri, Graham and me. She had never even met Graham, as he would meet us each day in the mountains.

The hotel has its own bakery next door, where the bread is baked fresh every day. Ireni, Nikos' enchanting elderly mother, serves behind the counter. One Sunday morning Mrs M observed that the bakery was closed. Ireni is very religious and was of course at church. One ding of the church bell and the bakery closes. The key is either left in the door or on the windowsill so that people can help themselves and pay later. Obviously the hotel has access to fresh bread at all times. This observation led to 'the bread this morning is stale'. Robin, who runs our photography courses, was staying at the hotel that day and said that he had been served fresh bread at breakfast. Peter, our very good friend who is nocturnal, lives two metres away from the bakery. He said that they were baking there at five o'clock that morning. The hotel owner has a farm and all the previous day's bread goes to his pigs, each of which incidentally used to be named after his waitresses. He had to stop this practice when they found out, but that is another story! It gave me great pleasure to inform the holiday company that at this hotel, stale bread is only served to pigs. The following day Mrs M's complaint was, 'the bread is too crispy and I have dodgy teeth so could you ask the baker to turn down the temperature of the oven?' The hotel manager very diplomatically suggested that she should just eat the soft part in the middle, adding that the owner would not mind, as the crusts would go to the farm. The manager then went into the kitchen and stuffed a tea towel in her mouth so that her screeches of laughter could not be heard in the restaurant.

Then came the greatest pleasure of our lives: buying a ferry ticket home for Mrs M. We always send our clients first class. If they leave at night they have a cabin, and for a day sailing they go into the lounge, as is clearly stated in our brochure. And so a new round of complaints were voiced. 'If I do not have a cabin, where am I going to put my luggage?' 'Do they have a first class lounge?' I should have said, 'No', but you can have a first class bench on deck', but I didn't. When the day came for her departure, flags were flying at the hotel, and all the guests and staff turned out to make sure she left. Nikos, the owner, was sobbing with relief. We were there two hours early to ensure that she didn't miss the ship, and the hotel had arranged for fifteen early calls for her. The band was playing, the church bells were ringing, the donkeys were braying. Then the news came that the ship had been cancelled. They had to give me a blood transfusion after I had slashed my wrists. We managed to cut down Nikos from the beam in the taverna where he was hanging. There was only one solution apart from a lengthened stay - the Skopelitis!

As previously mentioned, we try at all costs to keep clients off this fairground ride. Mrs M, along with all her other ailments, suffers from seasickness. With all the medication she takes, she can't take pills for this and relies on 'Sea bands'. We knew that on the Skopelitis she would need every Sea band ever produced. So with glee we drove her to the other port of Katapola to board said ship. On the way she asked about every bush and plant we passed and the history of every building. We must have passed this test, because our lack of knowledge was never mentioned in the subsequent letters of complaint. When we reached the port, the ship was sitting there in the protected bay, completely motionless. On the open sea that day, we knew it was force seven. We bought Mrs M and her companion drinks. She enquired, 'When do you think I should put on my Sea bands? 'Oh, I think as soon as possible', I said. We hoped that her friend was a good sailor, as he didn't seem to be concerned. We received no complaints about their return passage, so perhaps she was unconscious throughout. We watched the ship go over the horizon and returned to the hotel to drink champagne.

Then the written complaints came rolling in. 'The hotel restaurant wasn't part of the hotel.' (In fact, they are connected; it is only the stairs to the rooms that separates them.) 'The balcony to the room was too small to sit on.' (You can actually fit four chairs on it or two chairs and a table.) 'The walk down to the beach takes one and a half hours. (We walk it in eighteen minutes and most clients at a leisurely pace take twenty-five minutes.) She actually braved the bus back and according to her friend was a 'gibbering wreck' after this five-minute journey. I suggested that it was a shame she didn't try walking back up, as she would still be there on the beach and would have saved us all the subsequent administration.

The aggrieved Mrs M simply would not back down, and it finally ended up in court. All my replies to her complaints were read out complete with my sarcastic comments. At one point, when my comment about how they only gave stale bread to pigs was mentioned, she jumped out of her seat purple with rage and began screaming objections. The judge ordered her to sit down and be quiet because otherwise he would find her in contempt of court. We won. She paid costs.

To make us feel better after all these complaints the managing director of our agents in the UK sent us a list of complaints compiled by the British travel industry: 'You said that there was a hairdresser at the hotel. There was, but she was dead'. 'You didn't tell us that there would be fish in the sea. My children were frightened'. 'My girlfriend and I asked for single beds. You gave us a double bed and now she is pregnant'. 'We met some Americans on our holiday in the Caribbean. They had only to fly for two hours but you made us fly for eight'. I am sure that Mrs M's comments have now been added to the list.

Chapter XXXV Raki

What we really should have done was to tie Mrs M down and drip-feed her raki. Do you actually know what raki, or tsipouro, is? If you have drunk it you probably can't remember or were past caring! Essentially, it is a strong distilled spirit usually produced from the must-residue of the wine press (pomace). Thus, producing raki is an autumn activity. The name is dependent upon the area it comes from. In Turkey raki has an aniseed flavour, like Greek ouzo, whereas raki in Greece has no additives. It is just plain rocket fuel, containing approximately 45 percent alcohol by volume. The strength can vary enormously depending upon the temperature at which it is distilled. Although history is a little vague it appears to have been started by Greek Orthodox monks – well it would be wouldn't it! Records indicate that it was first produced during the 14th century on Mount Athos in Macedonia.

A considerable amount of raki is made on a small scale on Amorgos. A considerable amount of raki is also consumed on Amorgos. After making the wine, the pomace is put into large barrels and water added at a ratio of 70 percent 'gunge' and 30 percent water. These are sealed up and left to ferment for a month in the sun.

The fermented pomace is placed in a copper boiler which is traditionally heated from underneath, with a fire built from the prunings of the vines. The boiler has a long copper funnel which passes through barrels filled with cold water. As the hot steam is cooled, it condenses and liquidates. In approximately an hour, the warm raki begins to fall, drop by drop, on the other side of the funnel. The process lasts for many hours, indeed days, during which the owners of the boilers must taste for alcohol content, increase or decrease the heat and finally stop distillation when the raki has acquired the desired taste and strength. We always try to be on hand to assist with this arduous task and keep the distiller awake. The donkeys are still recovering from the time a certain hotel owner in Langada fell asleep and the raki overflowed into their field. You often see donkeys rolling on the ground but they usually get straight back up, not just lie there, with their feet sticking up in the air!

For years we had been using our ruin as an apotheki (store). Over one of the three rooms I had constructed a very leaky, plastic sheet covered roof. Every year in the spring, I had to go up there and patch it up. Every year I fell off. One year I didn't bounce and sustained injuries, albeit minor. In 2006 we decided to renovate that one room. The proper procedure is to contract an architect who draws up the plans and submits them to the authorities for planning permission. Get a lawyer, go to Naxos, fill in reams of paperwork, pay tax for now having a habitable room that is not a ruin and only then get in the builder. The very best master builder for renovations on our island is Andonis. He is in great demand and was available when I had scrapped myself off the ground. We scrubbed around convention and protocol and just sent for him.

Andonis is a very quiet, cool guy, not huge in stature, but well-built and strong. He is around 50, with a weather beaten face, shoulder length fair hair and clean shaven. 'I want a proper roof on that room' I said to him. He said, 'We will have to build up the walls to the original level before we can put a roof on'. I said, 'that's fine all the stones are there on the ground where they fell off, just where I fell off'. There was a scratching of head and a few murmurs as he assessed the materials required and the labour required. He said that he would charge around 1,500 euros. We shook hands and the work began the following week. In the end, it actually cost 1,800 euros, but he did much more work than we originally asked for and the result was spectacular. Goodness knows when it would have started if we had gone through the proper procedure. My logic had been that we were not putting in any windows or doors. We were not plastering the outside, we wanted it to still look like a ruin with the bare stone. The roof would only be seen from afar. Who was to know what we were doing in such a remote spot?

I didn't bank on the noticeable trains of donkeys bringing in the sand, cement, roof beams, steel banding, roof insulation and the builder's rather significant lunches. The agricultural policeman who is in charge of controlling such matters, along with many other things in the mountains, had better eyesight than I had counted on. He turned up when the work was in full swing. Henri was there, I was in the office in Langada. Andonis said to Henri, 'Just leave this to me'. It was explained that it was only going to be an apotheki, not an extra guest room. It was explained how it would look when it was finished. Andonis reasoned with the inspector over the protracted process that we would have to go through if we did it any other way than illegally. Relatively satisfied with our intentions, the inspector went away. This however didn't stop him from returning when the work was complete to ensure that we were all telling the truth. The matter has not been mentioned since, and we see the inspector very often down in the port or at festivals, when he is in full uniform carrying one of the icons.

There is no gate to the courtyard and no door on the apotheki. A few days after the store room was complete, I went in early one morning to get some firewood for our wood burning stove and there I found one very happy donkey ensconced inside. I said, 'we didn't build this for you! It is an apotheki, not a stable'. He just looked at me with those big wide innocent eyes, as if to say, 'Show me the legal documents to prove it'. Well, he had me there. We evicted him in the end, but we still have the occasional donkey wandering in when it is cold and wet. We do not mind. These sort of things are all a part of living in a remote village on the island of Amorgos.

Epilogue

The years rolled on. After completely leaving the UK in 2002, we rented out our house there. We sold it in 2006. Very little has changed on Amorgos since we moved here in 1999.There have been births, deaths and marriages. After a few minor strokes and then a major one, Amber died in her sleep in October 2008 aged 14. She is buried in her beloved olive groves next to our house in Stroumbos, complete with an impressive gravestone. We put flowers on her grave regularly, as do friends and previous clients who knew her.

Two years later Titi succumbed to lung cancer and emphysema. Henri helped to look after her on Amorgos where she was on oxygen for a few months in 2005. To our horror, she did not stop smoking, even when she was on oxygen. And despite her considerable medication, she did not limit her ouzo intake. She had to leave for France for permanent health care later that year. She died in 2010. She phoned me one afternoon in February that year, but all I could hear was heavy breathing. Not realizing that it was Titi, I put the phone down. I discovered the following day that it was her number on the call recorder and that she had died just a few hours after the call. If only I had known, at least I could have spoken a few words to her. We are confident that we will see her again one day and drink a few bottles of ouzo together.

For most people, one drastic life style change would be enough, and golly did we have some problems. Not for us. Since 2007, we had been going on safaris in Botswana, sometimes twice a year for a month at a time. You've guessed it! In January 2010, 'Special Interest Holidays International' diversified into Safari holidays in the Okavango Delta and we have moved into a house there. The plan is to spend six months on Amorgos over the Greek summer and six months in Botswana over the Southern African summer. This time, our rented house is on the side of a huge river, The Thamalakane, not the sea, which would be a bit difficult in Botswana. There is no road to the house, does this sound familiar? We have to drive seven kilometres across the bush to get there. The day after we bought our essential 4x4 Mitsubishi Pajero it broke down; where have I heard that before? To buy the car we had to get cash every day for ten days from ATMs using four different cards because the bank wouldn't accept our cards and wouldn't give us any money, I recall something similar. When we got to the house, the fridge was broken, yet again there was a feeling of deja vu. In week one I was in trouble with the police, another early introduction to the police station! OK it was only for speeding, in nearly forty years of driving I have never ever been caught before. It was not my fault, there are hardly any speed restriction signs. This did result in an open letter of complaint to the authorities published in the local newspaper from; 'Name and address supplied'. No crickets or rats, around the house but a resident crocodile called Charlie and a very noisy and temperamental hippo outside our bedroom window called Horace. There are many, many donkeys and goats. It is a parallel life style to Amorgos.

Most of this book was written with a cow's head sticking through the office window in Amorgos. It was edited in Botswana with, on one occasion a genet running up a tree right alongside me with a live boomslang (a large snake which produces one of the most potent venoms in Africa) dangling from its mouth. Summer temperatures can approach 50 degs so it is a little warmer than Greece but not a problem. Everyone says, 'you will find it difficult and frustrating living in Africa'. Not at all, it's all a very familiar experience, only this time it is; 'Out of the Fire into the Furnace'!

Acknowledgments

First and foremost, enormous thanks to my American editor Cynthia Cotts for her boundless encouragement and enthusiasm in turning my disjointed 'reports' into a comprehensible book. Her knowledge of Greek and Greece was invaluable.

My equal gratitude to British editor and publisher Richard Nicholls for his initiative and punctilious attention to the vagaries of the English language.

Last but not least, a huge thank you to my long suffering wife, Henri, for being a priceless part of all these exploits, if not instigator of some! Greater support hath no man.

About the Author

Paul Delahunt-Rimmer was born in 1955. He was educated at Chetham's School of Music in Manchester where he was awarded a Cathedral chorister's scholarship, going on to read Physics at The City University London and latterly gaining an MBA with the Open University Business School. He was commissioned into the Royal Air Force as a pilot in 1978 and served on 10 Sqn, 32 Sqn and The Queen's Flight. As an aircraft commander on the VC10 he flew the Royal family and government ministers worldwide. He also served in the Persian Gulf War. Retiring as a senior officer in 1994 he became an airline pilot and management consultant specialising in aviation and eco-tourism. He married Henrietta, also a retired Royal Air Force officer, in 1997. They lived in the Cotswolds in the UK and moved to Amorgos, Greece in 1999.

To learn more about the 'real' Amorgos and its hidden places see: Amorgos, A Visitor's and Walker's Guide, by Paul and Henrietta Delahunt-Rimmer (ISBN 978-0-9556288-2-5). Covering the flora, fauna and history of the island it contains many maps and colour photographs. It is available from the publisher www.travelleur.com and all good book suppliers.